OCEAN FRIENDLY CUISINE

Text & Art Direction

JAMES OLIVER FRAIOLI

✦

Consultant

MONTEREY BAY AQUARIUM

✦

Food Styling & Photography

TUCKER + HOSSLER

✦

Design & Typography

ELIZABETH WATSON

✦

Editors

TOM PETRIE

ANDREA DONNER

OCEAN FRIENDLY CUISINE

SUSTAINABLE SEAFOOD RECIPES FROM THE WORLD'S FINEST CHEFS

JAMES O. FRAIOLI

FOREWORD BY

JEAN-MICHEL COUSTEAU

WILLOW CREEK PRESS

Published by Willow Creek Press
P.O. Box 147, Minocqua, Wisconsin 54548

Library of Congress Cataloging-in-
Publication-Data
Fraioli, James O., 1968-
    Ocean-friendly cuisine : sustainable
seafood recipes from the world's finest chefs /
James O. Fraioil ; in association with the
Monterey Bay Aquarium.
        p. cm.
    ISBN 1-59543-061-X (hardcover : alk.
paper)
    1. Cookery (Seafood)   2. Sustainable
fisheries.   I. Monterey Bay Aquarium. II.
Title.
    TX747.F65 2005
    641.6'92--dc22

                        2004028309

Printed in Italy

To Cindy

whom I enjoy sharing the kitchen and my life with.

And to my agent

Andrea Hurst

who always believed in me.

CONTENTS

Preface by James O. Fraioli   11

Foreword by Jean Michel Cousteau   13

Introduction by Julie Packard   15
    The Seafood Watch Program   17
    Harvesting Methods   18

FRESHWATER 21

Rainbow Trout 22
Pistachio Crusted Rainbow Trout
    with Cilantro Citrus Hollandaise   24
Sautéed Mountain Rainbow Trout with Orchard Relish   24

Arctic Char 26
Arctic Char Brandade de Vendredi   29
Arctic Char with Oatmeal Crust   29

Catfish 30
Catfish Beignets with Remoulade Dipping Sauce   32

Crayfish 34
Crawfish Monica   37
Crawfish Etouffee   37

White Sturgeon 38
White Sturgeon Chowder   40
Seared White Sturgeon with Bok Choy and
    Shitake Mushrooms   40

White Sturgeon Caviar 42
Rosti Potatoes with Sterling Caviar   45
Cold-Smoked Fish on Endive and Apple
    Salad with White Sturgeon Caviar   45

Tilapia 46
Grilled Tilapia with Coconut Rum and Chili Glaze,
    Peppers, Baby Corn and Eggplant   48
Sautéed Tilapia Fillets with Lime and White Wine   48

SALTWATER 51

Northern Anchovy 52
Salad of Marinated Northern Anchovy, Heirloom Tomato,
Crushed Avocado, Arugula and Chilled Basil Dressing 54

Atlantic Herring 56
Pickled Herring served with Toast Points 59
Pan-Fried Atlantic Herring 59

Pacific Sardines 60
Pacific Sardines with Garlic and Balsamic Vinaigrette 62
Pacific Sardines Monterey Style 62

Pacific Cod 64
Sautéed Pacific Cod with Greek Walnut Salsa 67
Broiled Pacific Cod with Savory Rhubarb Sauce 67

Sablefish/Black Cod 68
Porcini Dusted Sablefish over Mussel Olive Oil Emulsion
with Roasted Young Bell Peppers and Elephant Garlic 70

New Zealand Cod (Hoki) 72
Serrano Ham-Wrapped Roasted Red Hoki with Aspao
Sauce and Olive-Oil Mache-Radish Salad over Rice 75

Dover Sole 76
Fillet of Dover Sole in Artichoke Bottoms 78

Sanddabs 80
Roasted Sanddabs with Meyer Lemon Relish 83
"Simmering Sanddabs" with Summer Vegetables and Pale Ale 83

Petrale Sole 84
Petrale Sole with Balsamic Butter Sauce 86
Petrale Sole with Sweet Onion, Heirloom Tomatoes and Thyme 86

Pacific Halibut 88
Pacific Halibut with Morel Mushrooms, Green Asparagus
and Truffled Yellow Split Pea Puree 91

Sockeye Salmon 92
Sake Glazed Sockeye Salmon with Miso Yuzu Vinaigrette,
Sesame Spinach and Crispy Noodles 94

Coho Salmon 96
Coho Salmon with Pistachio, Basil and Mint Butter 99
Wild Coho Salmon with Citrus Peppercorn Sauce 99

Chinook Salmon 100
"Sashimi" Grilled Copper River King Salmon with Wasabi Aioli
and Soy-Maple Drizzle 102
Baked King Salmon with Smoked Salmon Horseradish Crust
and Beurre Blanc 102

Spanish Mackerel 104
Spanish Mackerel with Lemon, Celery and Thyme 107
Baked Spanish Mackerel with Butter, Lemon and Paprika 107

White Sea Bass 108
Crab Crusted White Sea Bass with Green Onion Mashed
Potatoes, Fresh Asparagus and Sweet Red Pepper Sauce 110
Seared White Sea Bass over Grilled Vegetable Ragout
with White Truffle Oil and Fish Bordelaise 110

Striped Bass 112
Striped Bass with Orange, Thyme and Rum Mojo 115
Striped Bass Panamanian Style with Salsa Criollo 115

Albacore 116
Grilled Line-Caught Albacore on Ragoût of Wild Mushrooms,
Fiddlehead Ferns and Artichokes with Fresh Oregon Bay Shrimp
and Dungeness Crab 118
Warm Nicoise Salad 118

Yellowfin Tuna 120
Peppercorn Crusted Yellowfin Tuna with Saffron
and Fava Bean 123

CRUSTACEAN 145

Dungeness Crab 146
Dungeness Crab Cakes with Field Greens and Garlic Aioli 148
Dungeness Crab Club Sandwich on Toasted Brioche 148

Alaska Red King Crab 150
Marinated Alaskan King Crab Claws 153
King Crab Bisque 153

Snow Crab 154
Beer Steamed Snow Crab with Shallot Cream Sauce 156
Snow Crab Wrap Sandwich 156

Blue Crab 158
Soft Shell Blue Crab with Sake and Black Bean Sauce 161
French-Fried Jimmy Crabs 161

Florida Stone Crab 162
Curried Florida Stone Crab Claws with Hot Marmalade Dip 164

Green Mangrove Crab 163
Sautéed Mangrove Crab with Cilantro and Sweet Chili Sauce 164

Pink Shrimp 166
Carolina Shrimp Gumbo 169
Shrimp and Mango Summer Roll 169

Alaska Spot Prawn 170
Gamberoni alla Toscana 172
Stuffed Alaska Spot Prawns 172

California Spiny Lobster 174
Spiny Lobster Tail with Caviar, Seared Shallot
    Griddlecakes and Chervil Mascarpone 177
Spiny Lobster with Leek Tartar and Pickled Tomato 177

Maine Lobster 178
Maine Lobster and Avocado Salad with Red Wine
    Marinated Onion, Lemon Mayonnaise and Field Greens 180
Saffron Lobster Ramekins 180

Trevally Jack 124
Pan Seared Trevally Jack with Spicy Collards and
    Stone Ground Grits 126
Wok Charred Trevally Jack with Garlic Sesame Crust and
    Lime Ginger Beurre Blanc 126

Opah 128
Spicy Hawaiian Opah Fish Cake with Pineapple Aioli
    and Sweet and Sour Sauce 131

Mahi-Mahi 132
Seared Mahi-Mahi with Orange and Fennel,
    Polenta and Fried Leeks 134
Pan-Seared Mahi-Mahi with Shitake, Tomato
    and Fresh Salad with Jasmine Rice Cake 134

Wahoo 136
Grilled Wahoo with Key Lime-Cilantro Cream Sauce 139
Grilled Wahoo with Basil Vinaigrette and Hawaiian
    Avocado Relish 139

Wreckfish 140
Pecan-Crumb Crusted Wreckfish 142
Grilled Wreckfish with Jalapeno, Gouda Cheese Grits
    and Black Bean Mango Salsa 142

MOLLUSK & OTHER 183

Red Abalone 184
Sesame Mint Abalone in Lemon Shells 186

Abalone in Buerre Blanc with Tea-Stepped Raisins and Toasted Almonds 186

Clams 188
Linguine alle Vongole 191

Pacific Little Neck Clams in Butter and White Wine 191

Mussels 192
Curried Penn Cove Mussels 194

Mussels with Spicy Tomato and Chili Sauce 194

West Coast Oysters 196
Chilled Oysters with Roasted Poblano-Mezcal
Mignonette with Avocado-Cilantro Crema 199

Bloody Mary Oysters 199

Atlantic Bay Scallop 200
Coquille St. Jacques Montell 202

Live Atlantic Bay Scallops with Tarragon Butter 202

Atlantic Sea Scallop 204
Maine Sea Scallop Carpaccio 207

Grilled Sea Scallops with Romesco Sauce and Catalan Spinach 207

Market Squid 208
Charred Squid Skewers on Garlic Toast with Arugula 210

Day Octopus 212
Octopus with Green Papaya Slaw and Green Curry Vinaigrette 215

Grilled Octopus with Yuzu Soy Vinaigrette 215

Red Sea Urchin 216
Red Urchin "Uni" Shooter 218

Fresh Sea Urchin Roe with Lemon and Lime 218

Jellyfish 220
Spicy Jellyfish Salad with Endive, Smelt Eggs and Avocado 223

Sesame Marinated Jellyfish 223

Seafood Distributors 226

Acknowledgments 228

Photography Credits 229

Species Index 231

James O. Fraioli

PREFACE

In the early 1970s, swordfish, marlins, several tunas, and offshore groundfish like cod, haddock, and halibut—as well as many inshore gamefish—were half as plentiful as they'd been 25 years earlier. Today it is much worse. The journal *Nature* reports the earth has lost 90 percent of its large predatory fish species, such as cod, flounder and tuna. *Science* magazine published a startling discovery that revealed industrial fishing generally kills 80 percent of the fish in a given area within 15 years. Meanwhile, the U.S. Department of Agriculture estimates seafood consumption will jump seven percent by 2020. Only now, after irreparable damage has been done, are people starting to pay attention.

Whether or not to dine on seafood, and which fish to choose, are decisions that millions throughout the world make every day. Selecting species that are sustainable and caught without destruction of marine habitat or other species ("by-catch") are choices we should all be making, not just for ourselves but for the generations to come.

But does this mean the end of spectacular seafood flavor? That was the question I asked myself, and which led to this book. What I found was an amazing and growing army of compassionate fishermen and extraordinary chefs who care about what comes out of the sea, and who are creating a delectable world of sustainable seafood dishes. Great taste and responsible seafood choices definitely do go together.

During the course of assembling this book, I have learned that many consumers, including restaurants and seafood markets, still have a difficult time staying abreast of which fish are disappearing and which are doing fine. I further discovered that many of the corporate chain restaurants, several of which I have enjoyed since childhood, do not endorse sustainable seafood and would not support this book. I hope that this exciting cookbook contributes to the continuing education of all consumers, and helps develop a greater appreciation for our role as stewards of a sensitive environment.

I am grateful to have shared my gastronomic voyage with acclaimed food photographers, Jeff Tucker and Kevin Hossler, whose evocative images capture the true essence of seafood cuisine. I am also honored and privileged to have been able to work with the renowned Monterey Bay Aquarium and marine advocate Jean-Michel Cousteau, a role model whom I have admired and respected since I was a young boy.

The many glorious recipes featured inside represent a variety of styles and cooking methods—all graciously donated by leading chefs and organizations that support sustainable seafood. Before you begin to cook, take your time to read the recipe thoroughly, gather the necessary ingredients you need, obtain the appropriate seafood, and most importantly, enjoy the cooking process by simply having fun.

JAMES O. FRAIOLI

Jean-Michel Cousteau

FOREWORD

Some of the last, great adventures and mysteries on our planet exist at sea. Yet after decades of research, we have come to the conclusion that we don't yet know enough about the ocean to avoid the fact that we are affecting it at rates we never suspected. When my father co-invented scuba technology, he marveled at the beauty and the abundance he found and never suspected that in such a short time it could become so compromised by human activity for sheer pleasure, commercial profit, or even to feed the world.

Luckily for us all, Jacques Cousteau began diving with a camera in hand, having also pioneered some of the early underwater cameras. From that time on, we watched lobster marching one by one across the Caribbean sea floor. We saw groupers as long as men move slowly through Mediterranean waters, and dolphins bounded at the bows of our ships. We would never again look at the sea as a flat, static surface. On a deserted beach, my father said to me, "People protect what they love," and we had all fallen in love with the sea.

This love is in part because the ocean world is the last truly wild frontier. It is the last place where we behave as commercial hunters and go in quest of our prey. But, as in most parts of the world, we are too efficient at what we do.

In addition to commercial fisheries that we know are over fished and in trouble, we are now realizing that marine species are being exploited to extinction even on the deep sea floor; seamounts and corals that have grown slowly for thousands of years are being crushed by commercial trawlers; and natural products locked in deep sea habitats that could cure human illness are being lost forever. This fragile underwater wilderness, covering more than 50 percent of the Earth and 90 percent of the ocean floor, took millennia to grow, but is being destroyed rapidly by fisheries that are marauding the sea, scouring everything within their far reach.

The high seas are a veritable "old growth forest" of the ocean, and this deep ocean is an amazing cradle for millions of species, almost all still undiscovered. Approximately 98 percent of marine species live on, or just above the floor of the ocean. Two-thirds of all known corals inhabit these places.

Orange roughy, a deepwater fish and a fashionable item on restaurant menus, can take 20 to 30 years to mature, produce few large eggs, and can live to 150 years old. This species has been reduced to 16 percent of its original population by deep sea trawling.

So, we must support international coalitions to regulate all fisheries, including deep sea trawling, and to make them accountable. But most of all, we must become accountable for our own behavior and the choices we make as consumers. That is what this wonderful book is offering out of a love for the sea and a concern for its well-being.

My family and I have always operated from the principle that everything is connected. If indeed we protect what we love, then here is an opportunity to connect to the sea in a very meaningful way, and to spread the word every time you eat out or invite people in. It is a connection that begins the slow process of our giving back to what has always been the abundance of the sea.

JEAN-MICHEL COUSTEAU

Julie Packard

INTRODUCTION

Fish from the oceans were once viewed as an inexhaustible resource, able to fill nets and put food on our plates without limit for generations to come. But we're rapidly proving the old adage wrong: In the face of human demands, there just aren't enough fish in the sea.

The oceans are proving unable to keep up with a growing demand for seafood that is fueled by population increases and the industrialization of global fishing fleets. Recent scientific findings are sobering. Through our fishing efforts, people have eliminated 90 percent of the large fishes from the oceans. Today we're struggling to manage fish populations that are a fraction of their historic levels.

Yet there are still millions of boats, small and large, removing billions of pounds of fish from the oceans each year. Our short-term needs for protein and profit overshadow the most important goal: to manage fisheries to be sustainable in the long term. The impacts on our oceans have been devastating, in four main areas:

- Overfishing: We're taking fish from the water faster than they can reproduce. Today, more than 70 percent of the world's fisheries are at capacity, overexploited, or depleted.

- Bycatch: Each year, fishing fleets accidentally catch billions of pounds of unwanted marine animals, including sea turtles, sharks, young fish and seabirds. Snagged in gear aimed at commercial species, most are tossed overboard, dead or dying.

- Habitat loss: Vast expanses of seafloor are damaged by fishing gear, including trawl nets that plow the ocean bottom as efficiently as tractors in a field. Animals die, and the landscape is altered in ways that support less diversity of marine life. Even if the trawling stops, some habitats would need a century or more to recover.

- Illegal fishing: Unregulated fishing still plagues the high seas, where resource managers can't enforce catch limits and other regulations designed to ensure that fish populations remain healthy for the long term.

Aquaculture, or the farming of fish and shellfish, was once thought to be an easy solution—a way to alleviate pressure on wild species while meeting the growing demand for seafood. Unfortunately, the technologies of aquaculture advanced well before we understood the ecological impacts. Today, one-third of our seafood comes from farmed sources. And these systems are plagued with the same environmental impacts as industrialized animal rearing on land: pollution from animal waste and the spread of disease. The "Blue Revolution" has raised flags within environmental and scientific communities.

Fortunately, ecologically responsible fisheries and aquaculture operations do exist, and a growing sustainable seafood movement is working to make responsible fisheries standard fare for the future. The Seafood Watch program at the Monterey Bay Aquarium was created to help individual consumers, restaurateurs, and retailers to use their purchasing power to support these efforts.

Through Seafood Watch, we're working to shift consumer demand to support ecologically sound fisheries practices. Our pocket seafood guides and web-based background information promote seafood that consumers should buy and species to avoid, all based on the environmental sustainability of the source.

And it's working. Consumers are changing their buying patterns. Restaurants and retailers are offering sustainable choices—and teaching their customers about the importance of choosing sustainable seafood.

For us, it's not about limiting options. It's about identifying an abundance of great choices that are available and sustainable. Wild salmon, Pacific halibut, farmed tilapia, Dungeness crab, and shellfish

are all Seafood Watch "Best Choices." Think about how much thought people put into selecting the right bottle of wine at a restaurant, from scanning the wine list to talking with the server about possible alternatives. If we put half the effort into selecting seafood that we do into choosing the right wine, we'd be a long way toward assuring the future health of ocean wildlife.

And we are talking about wildlife—the last wildlife on Earth that we hunt on a large commercial scale for food. We have a chance today to save the ocean's magnificent top predators, many of which, like the tunas, are prized commercial catches. Or, we can stand by while they slide toward extinction like their terrestrial counterparts—the tigers, pandas, and countless less charismatic but unique species.

Because the concept for Seafood Watch is simple—people can make a difference for ocean wildlife through their seafood choices—it's having significant impacts. For example, two of our members were invited to attend a special dinner at Yosemite National Park. Chilean sea bass was on the menu—a species to avoid until its fishing operations no longer harm the marine environment. With our help, they wrote the park concessionaire explaining why Chilean sea bass and other species should not be on the menu in a place dedicated to preserving natural resources. As a result, the concessionaire took Chilean sea bass off the menu for that event. Then it went further, removing all "avoid" species from the menu at Yosemite and seven other national parks. This simple action is now helping to reach millions of park guests each year.

Today, millions of Seafood Watch pocket guides are being distributed. They can be found at Mount Rushmore, at Patagonia clothing stores, at community and co-op markets throughout the West, at zoos and aquariums nationwide, in corporate dining halls. The guides can also be quickly downloaded off the web, at www.seafoodwatch.org.

Using Seafood Watch guides, each of us can use our buying power as consumers to shape market demand. As we do, this demand will influence the supply, bringing more sustainable seafood into the marketplace.

We invite you to get involved in working toward a healthy future for our oceans. Learn more about sustainable seafood, share what you know, and most important, enjoy!

JULIE PACKARD
Executive Director
The Monterey Bay Aquarium

THE SEAFOOD WATCH PROGRAM

Consumers have the power to make a difference by the choices they make. To help with which seafood to select, this book has been assembled using those species which the Monterey Bay Aquarium considers "Best Choices" and those which should be purchased with "Caution."

Each species in this book has an easy-to-read Seafood Watch sidebar attached to its page, representing the Monterey Bay Aquarium Seafood Watch pocket guide. The color of the sidebar will be either green or yellow, indicating **Best Choice** or Good Alternatives.

Best Choices are fish which are abundant, well managed, and caught or farmed in environmentally friendly ways.

Good Alternatives are fish which consumers should think twice before choosing. There are some problems with the way the seafood is caught or farmed. However, these fish are better choices than those species which should be avoided.

When exploring this book, you may wonder why there isn't any mention of swordfish, farmed Atlantic salmon, orange roughy or Chilean sea bass. This is because those are fish which should be avoided, and such species are not featured in this book.

Avoid species are fish that come from sources that are overfished or are caught or farmed in ways that harm the environment.

It is okay to ask questions when shopping or eating out. Review the menu or seafood selection at the market. Ask the staff where their seafood is from. Is it farmed or wild-caught? How is it caught? If they are not sure, chose something else.

The Monterey Bay Aquarium updates the pocket guide at least twice a year. For the latest version of the card, or to learn more about sustainable seafood, visit www.montereybayaquarium.org or www.seafoodwatch.org.

Q. What is Seafood Watch? A program of Monterey Bay Aquarium designed to raise consumer awareness about the importance of buying seafood from sustainable sources. They recommend

BEST CHOICE	GOOD ALTERNATIVES	AVOID
Catfish (farmed)	Clams (wild-caught)	Caviar (wild-caught)
Caviar (farmed)	Cod (Pacific Ocean)	Chilean Seabass/Toothfish
Clams (farmed)	Crab, Blue	Cod (Atlantic Ocean)
Crab, Dungeness	Crab, imitation/Surimi	Crab, King (imported)
Crab, Snow (Canada)	Crab, King (AK)	Flounders, except
Crab, Stone	Crab, Snow (U.S.)	Summer/Fluke
Halibut (Pacific Ocean)	Flounders, Summer/Fluke	(Atlantic Ocean)
Lobster, Spiny (U.S.)	Lobster, American/Maine	Groupers
Mussels (farmed)	Mahi mahi/Dolphinfish/	Halibut (Atlantic Ocean)
Oysters (farmed)	Dorado	Monkfish
Salmon (wild-caught AK)	Oysters (wild-caught)	Orange Roughy
Sardines	Pollock	Rockfish (trawl-caught
Shrimp (trap-caught)	Scallops, Bay	Pacific Ocean)
Striped Bass (farmed)	Scallops, Sea	Salmon (farmed,
Sturgeon (farmed)	Shrimp (U.S. farmed or	including Atlantic)
Tilapia (farmed)	trawl-caught)	Sharks
Trout, Rainbow (farmed)	Soles,	Shrimp (imported, farmed
Tuna, Albacore	English/Dover/Petrale/	or trawl-caught)
(troll/pole-caught)	Rex (Pacific Ocean)	Snapper, Red/Vermilion
Tuna, Bigeye	Squid	(U.S.)
(troll/pole-caught)	Swordfish (U.S.)	Soles (Atlantic Ocean)
Tuna, Yellowfin	Tuna, Albacore	Sturgeon (imported,
(troll/pole-caught)	(longline-caught)	wild-caught)
	Tuna, Bigeye	Swordfish (imported)
	(longline-caught)	Tuna, Bluefin
	Tuna, canned (light)	
	Tuna, canned	
	(white/Albacore)	
	Tuna, Yellowfin	
	(longline-caught)	

How to use this guide

The seafood in this guide may occur in more than one column based on how it is caught, where it is from, etc.

Please read all columns and be sure to check labels or ask questions when shopping or eating out.

• Where is the seafood from?
• Is it farmed or wild-caught?
• How was it caught?

If you're not sure, choose something else from the green or yellow columns.

Choices for healthy oceans

You Have the Power
Your consumer choices make a difference. Buy seafood from the green or yellow columns to support those fisheries and fish farms that are healthier for ocean wildlife and the environment.

This Seafood Guide was last updated in November 2004.

This guide is updated regularly.

Visit www.seafoodwatch.org to download the latest version and Seafood Guides for other regions of the United States. You can also read seafood facts, learn about seafood and your health and much more...

MONTEREY BAY AQUARIUM

The contents of this guide are credited to the Monterey Bay Aquarium Foundation ©2004. All rights reserved. Printed on recycled paper.

Seafood WATCH

National Seafood Guide

which seafood to buy or avoid, helping consumers to become advocates for environmentally friendly seafood. They're also partners of the Seafood Choices Alliance where, along with other seafood awareness campaigns, they provide seafood purveyors with recommendations on seafood choices.

Q. How did Seafood Watch begin? Monterey Bay Aquarium developed a list of sustainable seafood as part of our 1997–1999 "Fishing for Solutions" exhibit anticipating visitor questions about making better seafood choices. Their Portola Cafe restaurant and husbandry department also adopted a "sustainable seafood" policy. The list evolved into the Seafood Watch pocket guide for consumers.

Today, with a grant from the David and Lucile Packard Foundation, they have a dedicated staff and funding to create and distribute regional Seafood Watch pocket guides across the United States and Canada.

Q. Why do seafood choices matter? Increased consumer demand for popular seafood is depleting fish stocks around the world and harming the health of the oceans. Today, nearly 70 percent of the world's fisheries are fully fished or overfished. Consumer purchasing power can support those sustainable fisheries and fish farms while relieving pressure on others.

Q. What is "sustainable seafood"? The Aquarium believes that seafood from sources, whether fished or farmed, can exist into the long-term without compromising species' survival or the integrity of the surrounding ecosystem, is sustainable.

Q. How does Seafood Watch develop recommendations? Seafood Watch pocket guides reflect what is sold in the regional market. Their current guide is for the West Coast. Next they will create guides for Hawaii, the Southern U.S., the Northeast, Great Lakes states, and the Midwest.

To create each guide, they establish partnerships with regional zoos and aquariums. Their staff does most of the research, collecting government reports, journal articles, and making personal contact with fishery and fish farm experts to create a Seafood Report. After a thorough review process, the information is run through their criteria for sustainability and a recommendation is developed. For more information about this process, please see Developing Sustainable Seafood Recommendations. Their regional partners assist with choosing the species to be researched and distribute the pocket guides to their guests.

Q. How does the Aquarium ensure accurate, up-to-date information? Their staff researches and evaluates each seafood item on their pocket guides. They work with fishery or aquaculture experts to gather pertinent information. Their research manager oversees the peer review process of our research reports. You can review their Seafood Watch resources online. You can also submit new resources online.

Using Seafood Watch is easy! Just follow these simple steps:

1. Pick up a **Seafood WATCH** pocket guide or download one from the Monterey Bay Aquarium's Seafood Watch Website (www.seafoodwatch.org).
2. Print out the card.
3. Fold up the card and keep it in your wallet or purse.
4. Take it out the next time you go to the market, a restaurant, or when you plan a catered event.
5. Choose a fish from the **BEST CHOICES** or **GOOD ALTERNATIVES** lists.

Commercial Harvesting Methods

Fishermen use many kinds of gear to catch the fish we eat. Here are some of the major methods used in commercial fishing:

Gillnetting. A gillnet is a curtain of netting that hangs in the water, suspended from floats. Gillnets are almost invisible to marine life and rely on this fact to catch fish. The spaces in the net are designed to be big enough for the head of a fish to go through, but not its body. As the fish startles and backs out, its gills get caught in the net.

Harpooning. A traditional method, harpooning is still used today to catch large bluefin tuna and swordfish. Fishermen known as "strikers" stand on a special platform that extends out from the fishing vessel. The striker holds an aluminum harpoon, 10 to 14 feet long, attached to a long rope.

The vessel's captain can use spotter planes to find the fish and angle his boat against the sun so the striker can get a clear shot. Once speared by the harpoon, the fish is quickly killed and hauled aboard. Harpooners return to dock the same day to obtain premium prices for their catch.

Longlining. Thousands of hooks all fish at once when a longliner rolls out the gear. The central fishing line can be 50 miles long, and it is strung with many smaller lines holding baited hooks. After leaving the lines to "soak" for a time to attract fish, longline fishermen return to haul in their catch. Pelagic longlining takes place near the sea surface, targeting midwater fishes like swordfish and tuna. Demersal, or "bottom" longlining, targets fishes that live closer to the seafloor, like cod, halibut, and sablefish.

Pole and Line. Fishermen stand shoulder to shoulder on the deck, each with a single pole and line in hand. It looks a bit like sport fishing—until the catch begins. Then it's clear that commercial pole-and-lining is extremely hard work. Fishermen with long poles and very short hooked lines catch the fish one by one and yank them out of the water. They whip the line overhead to bring the fish aboard, then give the rod a practiced twist to unhook the fish. The line is back in the water within seconds for another catch.

Tunas, mahi-mahi, and other large pelagic fishes are the target species. Some pole-and-liners use artificial lures. Some "jig" to attract the fish, jerking the line to simulate the motion of smaller fish. "Baitboat" pole-and-liners throw baitfish into the water, causing a feeding frenzy near the boat. Baitboats may also spray and splash the water surface, tricking the target fish into thinking there is even more feeding going on.

Purse Seining. A purse seine is a large net that encircles a school of fish. The bottom of the net is strung with a line that the crew can pull closed. Small boats move out from a mother ship to surround the fish with netting, like cattle in a corral. The bottom of the net is then pulled closed, like a purse (or a hiker's stuffsack). The baglike net is then raised up, trapping the fish inside it. Fishermen have traditionally used this method to capture sardines, herring, and mackerel, but purse seines are also used extensively for catching tuna.

Traps and Pots. Traps or "pots" are baited cages used to attract the catch and hold it alive until the fisherman returns. Often used for lobster, crabs, and shrimp, traps are also occasionally used to catch bottom-dwelling fish, such as sablefish or West Coast rockfish.

Traps are made of wire or wood. They have an entrance, a "kitchen" chamber where the bait rests, and a "parlor" section where undersized animals can escape through vents. Trap fishermen usually lay out many traps attached in a line. After three or four days, they haul their pots aboard, releasing any animals that are too small, too large, or not the right species.

Trawling/Dragging. Trawlers drag a cone-shapped net behind a boat. Different types of trawl nets are used to fish in the midwater (pelagic trawling) and along the seafloor (bottom trawling). Pelagic trawling is often used to catch large schools of small fish such as anchovies; bottom trawlers target bottom-living fishes like cod, halibut, and Pacific rockfish. Some bottom trawl nets are fixed with chains that slap the seabed, "tickling" fish into the net above. "Rockhopper" trawls are fitted with heavy tires that roll the net along rough, rocky seafloor. In dredging, a related form of fishing, nets with chain-mesh bottoms are dragged through soft sand to catch scallops.

Trolling. Long rods pull fishing lines behind a moving vessel in the method known as trolling. Fishermen use a variety of lures and baits to troll for different fishes at different depths. Trollers take speedy fishes that will follow a moving lure, such as salmon, albacore tuna, and mahi-mahi.

FRESHWATER

Rainbow Trout

Oncorhynchus mykiss

The U.S. Trout Farmers Association has developed a producer's quality assurance program for the entire trout industry. The quality assurance program monitors the farming and processing of trout to insure that consumers receive the safest and most wholesome products possible.

Rainbow trout are native only to the western streams of North America, ranging from Alaska to Mexico. In the wild, they are found in cold, clean waters of creeks, rivers and lakes. The average length of a rainbow trout is 12–18 inches. They are easily identified by the broad reddish band or "rainbow" that runs along their sides from head to tail. The reddish band blends into a dark olive green on the back and pure white or silver on the belly. The back, dorsal fin, and tail are generously sprinkled with black spots. A carnivorous fish, rainbow trout feed on a variety of organisms such as flies, crayfish, grasshoppers, beetles, and small fish.

Initially, rainbow trout were raised to replace wild trout stocks that were declining because of over-fishing, loss of habitat, and pollution. Trout farming expanded greatly in the 1950s, supported by the development of pelleted feeds, which reduced the cost of trout production.

Today, over 70 million pounds of trout, mostly rainbow trout, are grown annually in the U.S. Globally, the top trout producing countries are Chile, France, Denmark, and Italy. Available year around, trout found in U.S. markets is all farm-raised, mainly from Idaho, which accounts for over 75 percent of the production. Clear Springs Foods is the nation's largest trout ranch located in Buhl, Idaho—the Rainbow Trout Capital of the World. Improved production practices, selective breeding and nutritional feeds now make it possible to produce market size (10- to 14-ounce) trout in as little as 10 months.

Farmed rainbow trout are processed immediately after harvesting, and sold fresh or frozen to restaurants and supermarkets nationwide. Kept on ice, their shelf life is 10–14 days. Trout are marketed as gutted whole fish or as boneless fillets. The pinkish to red flesh is mild, delicate, and sweet.

✦ ✦ ✦

When it comes to selecting rainbow trout, the farmed variety is a smart and nutritional choice for a healthy diet. Trout contains the Omega-3 fatty acid, which helps reduce heart disease and lower cholesterol.

Seafood WATCH

All trout found in U.S. markets is farm-raised, mainly in Idaho and North Carolina.

Although trout are carnivorous fish, they are efficient at converting their feed into edible protein. To reduce their impact on wild fisheries, trout farmers are reducing the amount of fishmeal in trout feed. Farmed U.S. rainbow trout is a "Best Choice."

For current fishery status, visit www.seafoodwatch.org

Pistachio Crusted Rainbow Trout with Cilantro Citrus Hollandaise

CLEAR SPRINGS FOODS, Buhl, Idaho

◆

3 cups finely-chopped roasted and shelled pistachio nuts ▪ ½ cup chopped cilantro ▪ salt and pepper to taste ▪ 12 rainbow trout fillets ▪ ¼ cup fresh lime juice ▪ flour as needed ▪ 4 eggs, lightly beaten ▪ ¾ cup clarified butter ▪ **CITRUS HOLLANDAISE:** 4 egg yolks ▪ 2 tablespoons each of lime, orange, and grapefruit juice ▪ 1½ cups clarified butter ▪ ¼ cup chopped cilantro ▪ salt and pepper to taste

Stir together pistachio nuts and cilantro, add salt and pepper, reserve. Prepare Citrus Hollandaise by whisking 4 egg yolks with 2 tablespoons of lime, orange, and grapefruit juice. Whisk over a *bain marie* until sauce is light and fluffy. Away from heat, slowly whisk 1½ cups clarified butter. Season with ¼ cup chopped cilantro and salt and pepper to taste. Reserve and keep warm.

PER SERVING: Sprinkle 1 trout fillet with 1 teaspoon lime juice and dredge in flour. Dip fillet in egg and coat with reserved pistachio mixture. Place fillet (flesh-side down) on hot, lightly-oiled griddle or sauté pan. Drizzle fillet with 1 tablespoon butter. Sauté until just done, about 2 minutes per side. To serve: Place 1 or 2 fillets on each plate and top with Citrus Hollandaise Sauce. Serve with green salad and lemon and lime wedges. *Serves six to eight.*

Sautéed Mountain Rainbow Trout with Orchard Relish

CLEAR SPRINGS FOODS, Buhl, Idaho

◆

12 (6 ounces each) fresh boneless rainbow trout fillets ▪ all-purpose flour (as needed) ▪ ¼ cup butter ▪ ¼ cup vegetable oil ▪ **ORCHARD RELISH:** 2 cups diced red delicious apples ▪ ½ cup fresh lime juice ▪ 1 teaspoon grated lime zest ▪ 1⅓ cups diced red onion ▪ 1½ cups chopped toasted walnuts ▪ 1 tablespoon cider vinegar ▪ sugar to taste ▪ salt and pepper to taste

TO MAKE THE ORCHARD RELISH (4 CUPS): Combine all ingredients; adjust seasoning. Refrigerate 1 hour before service. Dredge the trout fillets in flour; sauté in 1 teaspoon butter and oil until just tender, about 2 minutes per side. TO SERVE: Place 1 or 2 fillets (depending on size) in center of plate and top with ⅓ cup Orchard Relish. *Serves six to twelve.*

Pistachio Crusted Rainbow Trout with Cilantro Citrus Hollandaise

Arctic Char

Salvelinus alpinus

In North America, Arctic char has been an object of commercial fishing since the 1860s. Today, char is farm raised to relieve wild stocks.

Today's chefs are finding plenty of ways to serve this little-known prize of serious fish lovers. With a succulent texture and a distinctive flavor somewhere between salmon and trout, Arctic char (spelled charr by some) is adored in certain circles even more than salmon. In Canada, Arctic char has become an official banquet food for many affairs of state and has even been served to the Queen of England when she's visited. Hillary Rodham Clinton requested Arctic char for the first state dinner hosted by the Clinton White House.

Although char is not as well known as various trout and salmon, chefs and gourmands agree: it's delicious. Thanks to an abundance of farm-raised Arctic char from Canada and Iceland, relieving the pressures of wild stocks, char is becoming increasingly popular—both in fancy restaurants and at home dining room tables.

Closely related to both salmon and trout, Arctic char exist in both anadromous (seagoing) and nonanadromous (freshwater resident) forms. Wild, anadromous char are found in the polar regions of North America and Europe, while nonanadromous char are found in landlocked waters in the United

Seafood WATCH

Although there is commercial and recreational fishing for Arctic char, aquaculture production is the primary source of Arctic char in the U.S. market. Iceland, Canada, Norway, and the United States are the primary producers of Arctic char, which demands a high price due to its limited availability. As Arctic char aquaculture uses more wild caught fish than it produces, the use of marine resources rates as a high conservation concern. This gives farmed Arctic char an overall ranking of "Good Alternatives."

For current fishery status, visit www.seafoodwatch.org

States, Canada, and several European countries. Arctic char are beautiful, silver fish with dappled pink along their undersides and brilliant shades of blue and green on their back and upper sides. Insects, mollusks, and small fish comprise the diet of Arctic char.

✦　✦　✦

Farm-raised char is available fresh year-round, whereas wild char hits the market for only a month or so in the fall. It is important to remember that when shopping for farmed char (the preferred choice) the color of the flesh varies dramatically from one farm to another. The flesh of Arctic char can be anywhere from dark red to quite pale pink, but should be clear and unmarred. Look for bright, silvery skin with white or pink spots and a fresh, clean scent.

Arctic Char Brandade de Vendredi

Arctic Char Brandade de Vendredi

CHEF RACHEL AUSTIN *in association with* **Northern Treasures, Yukon, Canada**

✦

2 fillets (4 oz.) Arctic char ▪ 3 Yukon gold potatoes ▪ 2 medium-sized yams ▪ 3 garlic cloves ▪ ½ cup vegetable oil
▪ ¼ cup milk ▪ 2 tablespoons butter ▪ 3 finely-diced bell peppers (assorted colors) ▪ fresh chives, finely chopped
▪ assorted field greens ▪ salt and pepper to taste

Peel potatoes and cut into chunks. Add to cold, salted water and boil until tender. As potatoes boil, roast the garlic cloves in hot vegetable oil until they are soft and golden in color. Drain potatoes and mash with roasted garlic. Add the butter, milk, and salt and pepper to taste. Mash until smooth and reserve. Peel the skin off the Arctic char fillets and break into small pieces; reserve. Peel the yams and slice paper thin. Fry the yam slices in hot vegetable oil until the edges are golden brown (this takes approx 5-6 seconds). Remove yam chips from oil and set on paper towel to drain. Sprinkle lightly with salt.

THE BRANDADE: Reheat mashed potatoes slowly (add a little milk if potatoes are too stiff). Stir in the chopped chives. Add Arctic char pieces and mix in gently. To serve: Place a dollop of brandade in center of plate. Top with a yam chip. Repeat until desired height is reached (approx 4 chips). Add piece of Arctic char to top layer. Garnish with field greens and diced peppers. Drizzle with olive oil. *Serves four.*

VARIATION: *Smoked salmon or trout can be substituted if Arctic char is unavailable.*

Arctic Char with Oatmeal Crust

CHEF BONNIE STERN, THE BONNIE STERN SCHOOL OF COOKING, Toronto, Canada

✦

2 pounds fresh Arctic char (fillets) ▪ ½ cup all-purpose flour ▪ 2 eggs ▪ 1 cup panko or homemade breadcrumbs
▪ 1 cup rolled oats ▪ 2 tablespoons chopped fresh parsley ▪ 2 tablespoons butter ▪ 2 tablespoons vegetable oil
▪ 1 lemon, cut into wedges ▪ salt and pepper to taste

Season fish generously with salt and pepper. Place flour in one shallow dish, beat eggs together in another, and combine breadcrumbs, oats, and parsley in another. To bread, dip each piece of fish into flour and shake off excess. Dip into egg and allow excess to drip off. Pat fish into oat mixture firmly on both sides. Arrange fish in a single layer on a rack set over a baking pan and refrigerate until ready to cook. Heat butter and oil in a large skillet. Preheat oven to 350°F. NOTE: Arctic char can vary in thickness and size. If the fish fillet is less than ¾" thick, cook 3 minutes per side in a skillet and don't bother finishing it in the oven. If the fillet is thicker, transferring to the oven will keep the fish moist. When butter/oil mixture stops sizzling and is just beginning to brown, add the fish (this may have to be done in batches). Cook fish (depending on thickness) and if need be, place fish on a baking sheet lined with parchment paper or foil, and bake 6 to 10 minutes. TO PLATE: Place 1 or 2 fillets on a plate and garnish with lemon wedges. *Serves six.*

Catfish

Ictalurus punctatus

Catfish can eat soybean and wheat pellets, reducing the demand on ocean fish used in fish feed.

Named for the long, cat whisker-like feelers found near its mouth, the catfish is a bottom-dwelling freshwater fish. Catfish can tolerate a wide variety of environmental conditions. They inhabit everything from tiny farm ponds and crystal-clear creeks to sluggish bayous, cypress-shrouded lakes, and broad lowland rivers.

There are more than 2,000 species of catfish, but the common variety found at seafood markets is the channel catfish. Native to North America and found from southern Canada to northern Mexico, channel cats are largely omnivorous and can grow to 50 pounds. Adults prefer deep water during daylight hours, moving into shallower water at night to feed. Favorite foods are insects, mollusks, crustaceans, salamanders, fish, and plant material.

Today, over 95 percent of the catfish found in retail markets is commercially farmed in 35 states, mainly in the South. By far, the most production comes out of Mississippi, followed by

Alabama, Arkansas, and Louisiana. Humphreys County, Mississippi—the "Catfish Capital of the World"—has long been the heart of the American catfish industry. Mississippi alone produces 75 percent of the catfish consumed in the U.S., and most of that comes from Humphreys County. The small percentage that is not farmed is likely wild catfish exported to the United States from overseas (i.e. South America, Vietnam). In supermarkets these imports are often on "special" and are cheaper, but bear little resemblance to U.S. farmed catfish. They also don't offer the flavor and consistency of their farmed counterparts.

❖ ❖ ❖

The commercial catfish industry ensures that American farmed catfish have a clean, mild flavor and firm texture by way of taste-tests done pond-side and at processing plants. Gourmet feed floats rather than sinks, keeping the fish from dredging the pond bottom and picking up a muddy flavor. The high-protein food pellets also cause them to grow much faster than their wild cousins. A 4- to 6-inch farm-raised fingerling reaches 1½ pounds in about 18 months. At this size the catfish are harvested with seines and taken alive to processing plants in aerated trucks. Once they reach the plants, the production process takes less than 30 minutes, making U.S. farm-raised catfish among the freshest fish available.

Seafood WATCH

Channel catfish, one of more than 1,000 catfish species, are the type most often farm-raised in the U.S.

Catfish can eat soybean and wheat pellets, reducing the demand on ocean fish used in fish feed.

Catfish farmers raise their fish in closed freshwater ponds. By carefully controlling the ponds' water quality, these farms can put catfish in the frying pan while protecting the environment. Farmed U.S. catfish is a "Best Choice."

For current fishery status, visit www.seafoodwatch.org

Catfish Beignets with Rémoulade Dipping Sauce

Chef Emeril Lagasse, *in association with* **The Catfish Institute, Indianola, Mississippi**

◆

1 pound U.S. farm-raised catfish fillets, cut into ½-inch pieces ▪ 2 tablespoons vegetable oil ▪ ½ cup chopped onion ▪ 1 teaspoon salt ▪ ½ teaspoon cayenne pepper ▪ 1 teaspoon chopped garlic ▪ ¼ cup chopped green onions ▪ 3 eggs, beaten ▪ 1½ cups milk ▪ 2 teaspoons baking powder ▪ 3⅓ cups all-purpose flour ▪ vegetable shortening as needed for deep frying. ▪ For the rustic rub: 4 tablespoons paprika ▪ 1½ teaspoons cayenne pepper ▪ 2½ tablespoons freshly ground black pepper ▪ 3 tablespoons garlic powder ▪ 1½ tablespoons onion powder ▪ 3 tablespoons salt ▪ 1¼ tablespoons dried oregano. ▪ For the remoulade dipping sauce: ¼ cup lemon juice ▪ 1½ cup vegetable oil ▪ ½ cup chopped onions ▪ ½ cup green onions ▪ ¼ cup chopped celery ▪ 2 tablespoons prepared horseradish ▪ 3 tablespoons creole or whole-grain mustard ▪ 3 tablespoons prepared yellow mustard ▪ 3 tablespoons ketchup ▪ 3 tablespoons chopped fresh parsley ▪ 1 teaspoon salt ▪ ¼ teaspoon cayenne pepper

Heat oil in a large skillet over medium-high heat. Add onion and sauté for 3 minutes or until slightly wilted. Season with ½ teaspoon of the salt and ¼ teaspoon of the cayenne pepper. Add catfish pieces and sauté for 2 or 3 minutes. Stir in garlic and green onions. Sauté for 1 minute. Remove from the heat and cool. Mix eggs, milk, baking powder and remaining ½ teaspoon salt and ¼ teaspoon cayenne pepper. Add flour, ¼ cup at a time, beating well until the batter is smooth. Fold in catfish mixture. Heat shortening in a deep fryer or large, heavy saucepan to 360°F on a deep-frying thermometer. Drop heaping spoonfuls of batter in the hot oil, one at a time. When the beignets pop to the surface, roll them around with a slotted spoon to brown evenly. Drain on paper towels. Sprinkle beignets with Rustic Rub and serve with Remoulade Dipping Sauce. For the rustic rub: Mix all ingredients in a small bowl until well blended. The rub mixture can be stored in an airtight container for up to 3 months. Makes about 1 cup. For the remoulade dipping sauce: Place all ingredients in a food processor and process for 30 seconds. Use immediately or refrigerate the sauce for several days in an airtight container. Makes two cups. *Serves four.*

Catfish Beignets with Rémoulade Dipping Sauce

Crayfish

Procambarus clarkii

From Maryland to Texas to Oregon, dishes featuring crayfish are growing steadily. It is estimated that crayfish production for food will double within the next 10 years.

Crayfish, also called crawfish or crawdad, are closely related to the lobster. More than half of the over 500 species of crayfish are found in North America, primarily in the Mississippi basin in Kentucky and Louisiana.

Nearly all crayfish live in freshwater, although a few survive in salt water. Crayfish are typical of most shrimp-like crustaceans in that they are characterized by a joined head and thorax (midsection) and a segmented body which can be sandy yellow, green, white, pink, or dark brown in color.

Crayfish often conceal themselves under rocks or logs. They are most active at night, when they feed on snails, algae, insect larvae, fish, and tadpoles. Crayfish have a pair of claw-bearing pinchers, which they use for cutting, capturing food, attack, and defense. Movement is a slow walk, but if startled, crayfish use rapid flips of their tails to swim backwards and escape danger.

Found in abundance in lakes and streams, crayfish average three to eight inches in length and generally live short lives, less than two years. Crayfish are harvested from both wild habitats (natural rivers, bayous, swamps, and lakes) and controlled, managed crayfish farms. The red swamp crayfish, from the Mississippi Delta in Louisiana, is the largest native species. White river crayfish, which are from northern Louisiana, and Pacific crayfish, which are found in Washington, Oregon, and California, are slightly smaller but have a similar taste.

✦ ✦ ✦

Only the tail meat from the crayfish is recovered during processing. The claw meat is tasty but very meager and difficult to pick out. The mild and succulent tail meat can be purchased fresh or frozen. Raw crayfish should be very active and alive when cooked because the meat in a limp or dead crayfish quickly spoils.

Crawfish Monica

Crawfish Monica

LOUISIANA CRAWFISH COMPANY, Natchitoches, Louisiana

❖

1 pound fresh crawfish tails, boiled and peeled ▪ ½ cup fresh oysters (optional), drained and quartered ▪ 1 stick unsalted butter ▪ 1 pint half-and-half ▪ 3 to 10 cloves of garlic, chopped (to your taste) ▪ 1 to 2 tablespoons Creole seasoning ▪ 1 pound cooked fresh pasta (use your favorite shape)

Cook pasta according to directions on package. Drain and rinse under cold water. Drain again, thoroughly, and reserve. In a large pot, melt the butter and sauté onions and garlic for 3 minutes. Add the crawfish tails (and oysters if using) and sauté for 2 minutes. Add the half-and-half and 1 to 2 tablespoons Creole seasoning until desired taste is achieved. Cook for 5 to 10 minutes over medium heat until sauce thickens. Add the pasta and toss well. Let stand for 10 minutes over very low heat, stirring often. **TO SERVE:** Serve immediately with hot French bread. *Serves four to six.*

Crawfish Étouffée

LOUISIANA CRAWFISH COMPANY, Natchitoches, Louisiana

❖

1 pound crawfish tails and crawfish fat ▪ ½ tablespoon flour ▪ 1 medium finely-chopped onion ▪ 1 to 1½ sticks butter ▪ 1 tablespoon finely-chopped bell pepper ▪ chopped green onion tops ▪ freshly chopped parsley ▪ salt and pepper to taste ▪ cayenne pepper to taste ▪ 2 or 3 cloves garlic, chopped fine

Melt butter in a large skillet. Add flour and salt until blended. Add chopped onion, chopped bell pepper, and garlic, and cook until tender. Add crawfish fat and cook about 10 minutes, stirring occasionally. Add crawfish tails and cover. Let this cook about 15 or 20 minutes on low heat, stirring occasionally. Add salt, pepper and cayenne pepper to taste, green onion tops, and parsley. Simmer covered until seasonings blend. Serve over rice. *Serves two to four.*

VARIATION: *Shrimp may be substituted for crawfish.*

White Sturgeon

Acipenser transmontanus

The white sturgeon is the largest freshwater fish in North America and can weigh over 1,500 pounds, be 20 feet in length, and live for over 100 years. It resembles some sort of prehistoric creature and is actually the modern relic of an ancient group of fishes that first appeared about 200 million years ago.

Worldwide, there are 29 species or subspecies of sturgeon, all of them found in the Northern hemisphere. Nine species are found in North America—two on the Pacific Coast. The Columbia River in Oregon is home to both Pacific Coast sturgeon species—the green sturgeon and the white sturgeon.

The white sturgeon is characterized by its large body size, long, cylindrical body, and a shark-like tail. Instead of scales, sturgeon are protected by a heavy, sandpaper-like skin and five rows of bony plates, called scutes, which serve as an armor-like covering. The white sturgeon can be dark to light gray, olive, or brown in color, and has a white belly.

Sturgeon have toothless, "vacuum cleaner" mouths capable of siphoning food. They generally feed on the bottom, rooting with their snouts and sucking up organisms that they detect with their

long, sensitive barbells. Their diet includes clams, mussels, crayfish, worms, and fish eggs. As the sturgeon grow larger, other fish become more important in their diet.

✦   ✦   ✦

A significant economic and cultural resource throughout the Northwest, white sturgeon became a heavily targeted fishery with major commercial landings in the Columbia River, wiping out much of the sturgeon population. Today, the majority of sturgeon found in U.S. markets is farm-raised. Farming sturgeon for meat and caviar is relieving the pressure on wild stocks of the endangered fish. In fact, the state of California has become the world's foremost producer of white sturgeon. As a pioneer in the farming of white sturgeon, Stolt Sea Farm has been raising Sterling White Sturgeon in the Sacramento Valley of California since the early 1980s.

White sturgeon is a nutritious delicacy that is available smoked or canned, as well as fresh or frozen whole steaks and fillets. Sturgeon meat is extremely firm but delicately flavorful.

White Sturgeon Chowder

STOLT SEA FARM, Sacramento, California

◆

1 or more pounds cubed, trimmed sturgeon ▪ 3 medium white potatoes, peeled ▪ 3 celery stalks, diced ▪ 1 large white onion, diced ▪ 4 large carrots, coarsely grated ▪ 1 bundle green onions, chopped ▪ 2 cans evaporated condensed milk (or fresh whole or 2% milk) ▪ juice of one lemon ▪ ¼ cup white flour (for thickening) ▪ ½ pound creamy butter ▪ salt and pepper to taste

Place potatoes, celery and diced onion in heavy 8-quart kettle. Cover vegetables with water and bring to a boil (kettle must be covered throughout the cooking process). Reduce to medium heat, allow to cook until potatoes are done but firm (to where you can insert a fork to the middle, but not so tender you break them in half). Reduce heat to medium/low for an additional 20-30 minutes before adding carrots, salt, and pepper.

Continue cooking until carrots are done (firm), before adding sturgeon cubes. Occasionally stir chowder through cooking process. Add milk, green onions, lemon juice, and butter. In a separate container, mix flour and water to a smooth paste (the more flour paste, the thicker the chowder). Slowly stir in flour paste until desired thickness. Ladle into soup bowls. *Serves six.*

Seared White Sturgeon with Bok Choy and Shiitake Mushrooms

STOLT SEA FARM, Sacramento, California

◆

Fresh white sturgeon fillets (6 oz. each, about 2"x 3") ▪ 2 teaspoons cracked coriander ▪ 6 tablespoons honey (divided) ▪ ½ pound soba or udon noodles ▪ 1 egg white ▪ 1 tablespoons minced scallions ▪ 1 tablespoon canola oil ▪ 2 tablespoons dry mustard ▪ 2 tablespoons champagne vinegar ▪ 1 tablespoon soy sauce ▪ 1 cup plus 1 tablespoon peanut oil (divided) ▪ 1 tablespoon black sesame seeds ▪ 8 baby bok choy ▪ ½ pound sliced shiitake mushrooms ▪ 1 teaspoon minced shallots ▪ 1 teaspoon minced garlic ▪ salt and pepper as needed

Season fish with salt and pepper. Grill, about 2 minutes on each side or until flesh is opaque. Combine cracked coriander in a bowl with 4 tablespoons honey; warm gently and brush mixture on fish. Blanch noodles in boiling water; cook until tender. Remove; plunge under cold water. Drain and cool. In a small bowl, whisk egg white until frothy. Add noodles, scallions, salt and pepper to taste, and toss well. Heat canola oil in nonstick sauté pan until smoking. Add noodle mixture and flatten immediately to form a ¼-inch-thick pancake. Cook 2 to 3 minutes on each side or until crisp and golden. Cut into 8 wedges; set aside. Combine mustard, vinegar, and soy sauce; whisk until smooth. Drizzle in 1 cup peanut oil; continue whisking until smooth. Stir in sesame seeds and 2 tablespoons honey; set aside. Heat 1 tablespoon peanut oil until smoking. Stir-fry bok choy, mushrooms, shallots, and garlic; cook until *al dente*. Season with salt and pepper. TO SERVE: Divide pancake wedges, 2 per serving, among 4 plates. Divide vegetables into 4 portions; place in center of each plate. Slice each fish fillet in half; place on top of vegetables. Spoon or drizzle sauce around inside of plate. *Serves six.*

White Sturgeon Chowder

White Sturgeon Caviar

Acipenser transmontanus

The United States is the world's largest importer of beluga caviar, accounting for 60 percent of the imports in recent years. Consumers can help the beluga sturgeon survive for many years to come by choosing great-tasting, farmed caviar varieties that are better for the environment.

Historically, 90 percent of the world's caviar has come from the Caspian Sea region and its tributary rivers. Three Caspian Sea sturgeon species produce three kinds of caviar: beluga, ostrya, and sevruga. These delicacies are imported from Russia, Iran, and Turkey. Unfortunately, the effects of pollution, loss of spawning habitat, increased poaching, and over-fishing has proven to be devastating to the sturgeon population and, consequently, caviar production.

Fortunately, a source closer to home produces an excellent alternative. Caviar from a small cousin of the Caspian Sea sturgeon, the white sturgeon, is being produced in American aquaculture farms in

San Francisco and in the Sacramento Valley of California. The American white sturgeon requires six to 12 years to mature before caviar can be obtained from them.

The caviar from white sturgeon has a slightly firm but delicate texture, with fine, distinguishable eggs. Color ranges from jet black to light gray, cream, and golden. The flavor of farmed caviar has been described as ranging from buttery to nutty, not too salty, and can be compared to the taste of the Russian Caspian Wild Osetra caviar.

✦ ✦ ✦

When buying caviar, make sure the berries (eggs) are whole, uncrushed, and well coated with the caviar's own glistening fat.

Proper storage for caviar is in the coldest part of the refrigerator. Caviar can be held as low as 26°F without freezing due to the salt content of the product. Never freeze caviar as the berries will burst when thawed, making the deteriorated product mushy. Once a fresh tin or jar of caviar is opened, it must be consumed within a couple of days.

When serving caviar from a container, always place the container on a bed of ice to keep the eggs cold and only use nonmetallic utensils. Metal, especially silver utensils, may impart a metallic taste to the caviar.

Rosti Potatoes with White Sturgeon Caviar

Rosti Potatoes with White Sturgeon Caviar

CHEF KEN FRANK, LA TOQUE RESTAURANT, Napa California, *in association with* **Stolt Sea Farm, California**

◆

¼ cup crème fraîche (see below) ▪ juice of ¼ fresh lemon ▪ 1 heaping teaspoon chopped fresh chives or 3 turns freshly-ground white pepper ▪ 2 medium russet potatoes ▪ ½ cup peanut oil ▪ 1 to 2 ounces farmed sturgeon caviar

MAKING CRÈME FRAÎCHE: Stir together 1 part fresh buttermilk and 4 parts heavy cream. Let sit and cure for 8 hours at room temperature, then refrigerate overnight to allow it to thicken. The crème fraîche will keep for 10 days to 2 weeks in the refrigerator. Devon cream or sour cream can be substituted for crème fraîche. Mix together the crème fraîche, lemon juice, and chives or pepper in a small bowl. Let rest for 1 to 2 hours at room temperature to allow crème fraîche to thicken. Scrub the potatoes —they need not be peeled—and grate them on the coarsest side of a cheese grater. Form the shredded potatoes into 4 small patties— loosely, don't press them—about ½-inch thick. Prepare right away, as shredded potatoes will blacken. Heat ⅛-inch peanut oil in a sauté pan over moderate heat so that a test shred of potato sizzles. Using a spatula, carefully place the patties in the hot oil and fry them until they are golden brown on both sides (approx 2 to 2½ minutes per side). Remove patties and blot excess oil with paper towel. TO SERVE: Top each potato patty with the crème fraîche, top with caviar, and serve immediately. *Serves four.*

Cold-Smoked Fish on Endive and Apple Salad with White Sturgeon Caviar

CHEF CRAIG VON FOERSTER, SIERRA MAR RESTAURANT, Big Sur, California, *in association with* **Stolt Sea Farm, Sacramento, California**

◆

12 ounces unflavored, soft goat cheese ▪ 4 ounces hazelnuts, toasted, peeled, and coarsely chopped ▪ 2 Gala, Fuji or Braeburn apples, cored ▪ 2 teaspoons canola or vegetable oil ▪ 2 teaspoons sugar ▪ 2 endive, leaves cut lengthwise into thin strips ▪ 12 slices (about 10 oz.) cold-smoked fish (such as sturgeon or salmon) ▪ 1½ ounces white sturgeon caviar ▪ APPLE VINAIGRETTE: 2 cups apple juice ▪ ¼ cup apple cider vinegar ▪ 1 shallot, finely chopped ▪ ½ teaspoon salt ▪ ⅛ teaspoon pepper ▪ ½ cup canola oil ▪ 2 tablespoons hazelnut or pumpkin seed oil

Form goat cheese into 6 round patties. Coat on all sides with chopped hazelnuts. Refrigerate until serving. FOR THE APPLE VINAIGRETTE: In a saucepan, cook apple juice until reduced to ½ cup (about 20 minutes). While syrup is warm, stir in vinegar, shallots, salt and pepper. Gradually whisk in oils. Taste and adjust seasonings. Reserve. Cut 1 of the apples into 6 slices. Lightly brush with oil and sprinkle with sugar. Grill or sauté apples in nonstick skillet until golden on one side, about 2 minutes. Turn, cook on second side until crisp-tender, about 2 minutes. Cut remaining apple into thin strips. Toss with the endive and ¾ cup of the vinaigrette. TO SERVE: Place 1 cup apple and endive mixture on salad plate. Arrange 1 apple slice, 1 goat cheese patty, and 2 slices smoked fish on endive mixture. Sprinkle with about 1 teaspoon caviar. Drizzle some of the vinaigrette around the edge of the plate. If desired, garnish plate with additional toasted hazelnuts, apple slices, and whole endive leaves. *Serves six.*

Tilapia

Oreochromis spp.

Tilapia is the fastest growing aquaculture crop in the United States and around the world. According to the American Tilapia Association, tilapia is now the eighth most popular seafood consumed in the U.S.

Tilapia is native to Africa, but after its successful introduction to Arizona for aquaculture in the 1960s, it is now farmed in ponds and tanks worldwide. As strange as it may sound, much of the farmed tilapia found in today's U.S. markets comes from Columbia and Costa Rica, while American-raised tilapia is sold overseas as a live product. Farmers in Taiwan, Thailand, and Indonesia also export frozen product to the U.S.

Tilapia are four to 18 inches long, weigh six ounces to over five pounds, and come in a variety of colors (orange, red, white, gray, or blue). Much of the tilapia aquaculture production is harvested at one to one-and-one-half pounds.

Tilapia are favored for fish farming because of their high growth rate and frequent spawning tendencies. They are also a hardy, freshwater fish that tolerate a wide range of water conditions, making them easy to raise. Tilapia farms utilize enclosed systems and water controls to prevent water pollution, escapes, and conflicts with other wildlife. More than 300,000 tons of tilapia is produced

worldwide every year, and the fish can be found in markets year-round due to the consistent supply from fish farms. Tilapia thrive on inexpensive, vegetable-based foods, making them a good source of eco-friendly protein. Tilapia aquaculture has one of the least environmental impacts of any farmed fish.

✦ ✦ ✦

Tilapia meat is typically white, although meat from the red-skinned tilapia may have a reddish tint. Cooked meat is opaque. A brown colored meat will result from red-skinned fish if the tilapia is not skinned deeply enough. The firm, flaky texture of tilapia has a sweet, mild flavor due to the high-quality, grain-based pellets they are fed.

Fresh tilapia meat should be moist and resilient. It should have no musky odor. Do not buy frozen tilapia that has freezer burn. If mushy when thawed, discard. Tilapia absorbs flavor from the water in which it is raised, so check the source. Shelf-life for fresh tilapia is two weeks. Shelf-life for frozen product is six months. Blast frozen or block frozen is a sign of a poor product.

Tilapia can be broiled, fried, grilled, baked, poached, sautéed, or steamed. Tilapia's attractive skin may be displayed, but should not be eaten due to its bitter flavor.

Seafood WATCH

Native to North Africa, tilapia are farm-raised all over the world. Tilapia are hardy, freshwater fish that tolerate a wide range of water conditions, making them easy to raise.

In the U.S., most tilapia are farmed in inland re-circulating systems that have little impact on the environment. Tilapia thrive on inexpensive vegetable-based foods, making them a good source of eco-friendly protein. Farm-raised tilapia is a "Best Choice."

For current fishery status, visit www.seafoodwatch.org

Grilled Tilapia with Coconut Rum and Chili Glaze, Peppers, Baby Corn and Eggplant

Chef H. Lamar Thomas, East West Bistro, Athens, Georgia

◆

4 fresh tilapia fillets (6 ounces each) ▪ 8 ounces hickory chips soaked in water for a day ▪ 8 ounces mesquite chips soaked in water for a day ▪ 1 red bell pepper, cut in fourths ▪ 1 green bell pepper, cut in fourths ▪ 1 eggplant, sliced into 8 slices (optional) ▪ 1 tablespoon extra virgin olive oil ▪ 1 tablespoon course salt ▪ 4 ears of fresh corn, in husks (soaked in water for 30 minutes prior to grilling) ▪ For the coconut rum and chili glaze: 1 tablespoon chili paste (or substitute with one minced jalapeno pepper, 1 teaspoon minced fresh garlic, and 2 tablespoons rice vinegar) ▪ 4 ounces crushed cashews ▪ 4 ounces coconut rum ▪ 3 ounces Worcestershire sauce ▪ 3 ounces maple syrup

Begin by preparing the Coconut Rum and Chili Glaze: Combine chili paste and crushed cashews, and toast on medium heat until it begins to smoke. Then add the coconut rum, Worcestershire sauce, and maple syrup. Turn the heat up to medium-high and cook for 5 minutes. Gently stir with a wooden spoon as it cooks. When the sauce is ready, it will be thick enough to coat the spoon when lifted from the sauce. To grill the fish: When the charcoal briquettes are half gray, add 8 ounces hickory chips and 8 ounces mesquite chips. Let the chips cook about 10 minutes; they will be smoldering and turning red. Rub the grill screen with peanut oil or corn oil. Grill the bell peppers and corn in the husks. Before adding the eggplant (optional), press the eggplant between paper towels to drain excess liquids and oils. Place eggplant on grill. While vegetables cook, add the tilapia fillets. Cook the fish 10 minutes per side, turning several times. Brush the fish with 1 tablespoon of the glaze after each turn. To serve: place one grilled tilapia fillet on top of several pieces of grilled bell peppers along with an ear of corn. *Serves four.*

Sautéed Tilapia Fillets with Lime and White Wine

Pacific Seafood Group, Clackamas, Oregon

◆

1 to 1⅓ pounds fresh tilapia fillets, about ½-inch thick ▪ 3 tablespoons all-purpose flour ▪ 1 clove minced garlic ▪ ½ cup dry white wine ▪ 1 tablespoon lime juice ▪ ½ tablespoon butter, plus 1 tablespoon butter ▪ 1 tablespoon olive oil ▪ 3 green onions, chopped ▪ salt and pepper to taste

Rinse the fish and pat dry. Put the flour on a plate and season fish with salt and pepper. Dredge the fillets in the flour, patting to remove excess. In a small bowl, combine the garlic, wine, lime juice and butter. Reserve. Heat the oil in a large sauté pan over medium-high heat. Add the fillets without overlapping (you may need to cook in 2 batches). Cook until golden on the bottom, about 3 minutes. Turn the fillets over and cook until opaque through the thickest part, 1 to 2 minutes more. Transfer the fish to a platter and keep warm (cover with foil or place in a 200°F oven). Add the wine/lime mixture to pan and boil, scraping up cooked bits, until reduced by half, 2 to 3 minutes. Stir in the green onions and heat on low for about 30 seconds. To serve: Pour the sauce over the fish and serve immediately. *Serves four.*

Grilled Tilapia with Coconut Rum and Chili Glaze, Peppers, Baby Corn and Eggplant

SALTWATER

Northern Anchovy

Engraulis mordax

The Northern anchovy is commercially fished from British Columbia to Mexico, primarily from San Francisco, south. It was not commercially important until after the collapse of the Pacific sardine.

The Northern anchovy is a small silvery fish with a blue or green back. They have a very large mouth which they often keep open while swimming, allowing an increased amount of water to enter through the gills producing more oxygen. Anchovies are an important food source for various species of seabirds and marine mammals as well as many species of fish, including rockfish, tuna, shark, and salmon.

The Northern anchovy is distributed from Canada to the Gulf of Mexico. Adults are pelagic and are found in estuaries, near-shore areas, and out as far as 100 miles offshore in depths from over 150 fathoms right up to the surface. Juveniles are also pelagic and abundant in shallow, near-shore areas and estuaries. Like sardines, adult and juvenile anchovies form tightly-packed schools as an adaptation against predators. The maximum length for a Northern anchovy is about seven inches.

Northern anchovies feed primarily during the day, consuming planktonic crustaceans and fish larvae either by filter feeding or biting, depending of the size of the food. Females need to eat approximately four to five percent of their wet weight per day for growth and reproduction.

The Northern anchovy is extremely abundant and commercially fished from British Columbia to Mexico, primarily off San Francisco and south. It was not commercially important until after the Pacific sardines declined due to a severe climate change.

Anchovies are harvested using large seine nets. They are turned primarily into fish meal and oil for fertilizer and animal feed, although they are also a popular bait fish. A minor percentage of Northern anchovies are processed for human consumption, in pickled or salted forms or as fish oil.

The Northern anchovy is available year-round in both fresh and frozen forms. Anchovies should have a pleasant, strong aroma; if their smell is disagreeable, it's a sure sign they've gone bad.

✦ ✦ ✦

Choose anchovies packed in olive oil for the best flavor; the ones in glass jars tend to taste better than canned. If you find them too salty, soak them in cold water for about 20 minutes and pat them dry with paper towels.

Salad of Marinated Northern Anchovy with Heirloom Tomato, Crushed Avocado, Arugula and Chilled Basil Dressing

CHEF CORNELIUS GALLAGHER, OCEANA RESTAURANT, New York, New York

✦

16 northern anchovy fillets ▪ 1 beefsteak tomato, peeled and seeded, cut into 8 wedges ▪ ¼ cup red onion, peeled and thinly sliced ▪ 3 tablespoons olive oil ▪ 3 tablespoons red wine vinegar ▪ 2 tablespoons Italian parsley, sliced ▪ ⅓ cup basil leaves ▪ ¼ cup vegetable oil ▪ 2 tablespoons toasted pine nuts ▪ 1 clove garlic, peeled ▪ 1 tablespoon grated Parmesan cheese ▪ 1 avocado, peeled and seeded ▪ 1 teaspoon lemon juice ▪ 1 teaspoon cumin powder ▪ 1 cup arugula leaves ▪ salt and pepper to taste

Combine tomato wedges, red onion, olive oil, red wine vinegar, and parsley in a large bowl, toss well, and season with salt and pepper. Cover bowl and refrigerate overnight, gently stirring the tomatoes from time to time. The following day, drain the tomatoes, reserving the juices. Separate the tomatoes and red onions, reserve. Fillet and de-bone the anchovies (if need be). Add the anchovies to the reserved tomato juices, cover, and reserve in the refrigerator. In a blender, combine the basil, vegetable oil, pine nuts, garlic, and Parmesan cheese, cover and purée until smooth. Transfer the blender jar to the refrigerator and reserve.

In a medium-sized mixing bowl, combine the meat from the avocado with the lemon juice and cumin, and season to taste with salt and pepper. Crush the avocado lightly with the back of a fork, mixing until just combined. Transfer the anchovies to a plate and combine the tomato juices with the basil purée, chill until ready to serve. TO SERVE: Spoon one fourth of the avocado into the center of four chilled plates. Arrange four anchovy fillets on top of the avocado, and spoon one quarter of the reserved tomato and red onion pieces around them. Drizzle the chilled basil-tomato purée around the plate, and garnish with arugula leaves. *Serves four.*

Salad of Marinated Northern Anchovy with Heirloom Tomato, Crushed Avocado, Arugula and Chilled Basil Dressing

Atlantic Herring

Clupea harengus

Atlantic herring fisheries existed as early as 240 A.D. Nearly every culture along North Atlantic coasts, from historical tribes and settlements to modern communities, have fished for herring.

The *Guinness Book of World Records* states that the Atlantic herring is considered the world's most numerous fish. When herring migrate, they can run in schools extending 17 miles and containing millions of fish. There are more than 180 species in the herring family, including sardines and anchovies.

The Atlantic herring is a small plankton-feeder that grows to a maximum of 17 inches and one-and-one-half pounds. Distinguishing characteristics include a dorsal fin located midway along the body and a saw-toothed keel along the belly. The fish is iridescent, greenish or grayish blue dorsally with a silvery abdomen and sides. If viewed at close range, the Atlantic herring can be positively identified by its conspicuous cluster of small teeth arranged in an oval shape on the roof of its mouth. No other herring species possesses this distinctive circle of teeth.

Atlantic herring are an abundant, pelagic fish that inhabit the open sea and offshore banks for most of their lives. In the spring and summer, young juveniles are numerous in inshore waters along the Maine coast. Adults migrate across hundreds of miles of ocean during their life spans. In the winter, schools of migrating Atlantic herring can join forces, forming massive expanses of fish stretching as far as the eye can see.

Seafood WATCH

While Atlantic herring was subject to heavy fishing pressure in the 1960s, the populations have now recovered and appear to be healthy. Management has been effective at maintaining the stocks at a healthy level and enforcing regulations. The combination of these factors results in an overall ranking of "Best Choice" for Atlantic Herring.

For current fishery status, visit www.seafoodwatch.org

Just as marine birds and mammals have taken advantage of bountiful herring schools along northern coasts, humans have long depended upon this resource for sustenance. Nearly every culture along North Atlantic coasts, from historical tribes and settlements to modern communities, have fished for herring.

Today, in the Gulf of Maine, herring are harvested primarily by purse seiners and mid-water trawlers, which produce very little bycatch. The herring fishery supports a multi-million dollar a year canning industry in Maine and Atlantic Canada.

✦ ✦ ✦

The sardine canneries in Maine, New Brunswick, and most of the North Atlantic states exclusively process young Atlantic herring. In other locations, however, a can labeled "sardines" may contain an entirely different type of fish. The Pacific sardine *(Sardinops sagax)*, or pilchard, is the fish that inspired "Cannery Row" in Monterey, California—immortalized by American writer John Steinbeck. While the fish share the same family and some-times the same name on a can label, Atlantic herring and Pacific sardines are two distinct species.

Pickled Herring served with Toast Points

Pickled Herring served with Toast Points

KARL FRANTZ *in association with* **Puget Sound Anglers, Anacortes, Washington**

◆

Fresh herring (amount as needed) ▪ rock salt (as needed) ▪ 2 lbs. brown sugar ▪ 3 quarts cider vinegar ▪ 2–3 white onions (chopped or sliced) ▪ 1½ jars of 1.5 oz Pickling Spice (Pickling spice consists of 2 teaspoons whole black peppercorns, 2 teaspoons yellow mustard seeds, and 1 teaspoon each of crushed chilies, bay leaves, allspice berries, fennel seed, dill seed, whole cloves, and ginger, which yields approx. ¼ cup)

In a large glass container (non-metallic) or crock pot, layer rock salt and herring skin side down until desired amount is achieved. Cover last layer of herring with rock salt. Weigh down layers with a heavy object. Store container in a cool place (garage or refrigerator) for 7 days. Remove herring and rock salt and rinse out container. Fill container with cold fresh water. Add the herring and soak for 24 hours. Remove herring and rinse out container. To the empty container, add the brown sugar, cider vinegar, onions, and pickling spice. Add the herring and soak for 5-7 days in a cool place. Stir daily. TO SERVE: Pour pickled herring in a bowl or deep dish and serve with toast points as an appetizer.

Pan-Fried Atlantic Herring

DEPARTMENT OF FISHERIES AND AQUACULTURE, GOVERNMENT OF NEWFOUNDLAND & LABRADOR, St. Johns, Newfoundland

◆

1 or 2 large fresh Atlantic herring ▪ ½ cup flour (seasoned with salt and black pepper to taste) ▪ 3 tablespoons cooking oil ▪ 1 egg ▪ lemon wedges for garnish

Beat egg lightly in a bowl. Dip the herring into egg and roll in the seasoned flour. Shake off excess and set aside. Heat the oil in a skillet at medium temperature. Cook herring until the flesh starts to flake. TO SERVE: Plate the herring and garnish with lemon wedges. If desired, accompany with sliced bell peppers and red potatoes. *Serves two.*

Pacific Sardine

Sardinops sagax

California indicates that sardines undergo natural fluctuations of high and low abundance varying in length between 50 to 75 years, apparently related to large-scale climate change.

Sardines are small, silvery fish with a single dorsal fin located over the middle of the body, a forked caudal fin, and a keel of large, spiny scales along the belly.

The name derives from the isle of Sardinia, where the fish—a species of pilchard in the herring family—were originally caught and cooked.

In times of abundance, sardines commonly occur up to 150 miles offshore. They are migratory and may travel thousands of miles between feeding and spawning habitats over the course of a year. They are coastal, pelagic fish and travel in schools that may contain hundreds of thousands to millions of individual fish. The large numbers of fish in the schools and their rapid, coordinated movements

Seafood WATCH

These fish reproduce rapidly and travel in gigantic schools, but their success depends strongly on a favorable marine environment. Today, sardines have made a comeback on both coasts – good news for people who enjoy these tasty little fish, and for the many kinds of sea birds, sea mammals, and large fish that feed on sardines. Pacific Sardines are a "Best Choice."

For current fishery status, visit www.seafoodwatch.org

serve as an adaptation against predators. Sardines feed on zooplankton and phytoplankton by filter feeding and selective capture of larger prey.

Due to a severe climate change in the 1960s that brought cooler waters into the eastern North Pacific, resulting in loss of habitat, the Pacific sardines neared extinction. This heavily affected the commercial sardine fishery which counted on the fish for fish meal and oil, as well as for canned products for human consumption. The history of the sardine fishery followed a now-familiar pattern of rapid growth and accelerating decline, like virtually all other fisheries around the world based on small, pelagic fish.

A major sardine fishery was developed in the Gulf of California during the 1970s and has persisted to the present, with much improved habitat conditions due to favorable ocean conditions. Today, the Pacific sardine, which is harvested with large seine nets, has returned to abundant numbers and is well regulated by the California fishery.

✦ ✦ ✦

Fresh sardines have a nutty, slightly sweet taste. They are available seasonally at fish markets but are highly perishable and should be stored immediately on ice and cooked the same day. Much of the canned sardines from the Atlantic coast, (U.S. and Canada), which last indefinitely, are actually Atlantic herring. The Pacific herring is used mostly as bait, but small quantities are available fresh. In 2002, a sardine cannery opened in Salinas, California, offering canned Pacific sardines.

Sardines with Garlic and Balsamic Vinaigrette on Toasted Sourdough

CHEF ALICE DOYLE, DOYLES PALACE HOTEL, Sydney, Australia

✦

2 to 3 pounds of fresh sardines, filleted with heads and backbones removed ▪ cold water (as needed) ▪ sea salt (as needed) ▪ 4 large bay leaves ▪ 4 sticks celery, finely chopped ▪ 12 black peppercorns, crushed ▪ 1 brown onion, chopped ▪ ½ lemon, chopped skin and all ▪ FOR THE GARLIC AND BALSAMIC VINAIGRETTE: 1 clove garlic, crushed and finely chopped ▪ 1 cup olive oil ▪ ½ teaspoon sugar ▪ 1 teaspoon salad herbs ▪ 2 tablespoons balsamic vinegar ▪ sea salt and fresh ground black pepper to taste ▪ fresh toasted sourdough bread (as needed)

Place filleted sardines in a strainer and rinse under cold water, being careful not to break the fillets. Place fillets in a large, heavy pan and cover with water. Add salt and remaining ingredients, slowly bring to a boil, lower heat and simmer for 5 minutes. Cool in pan, then gently remove fillets and reserve. FOR THE VINAIGRETTE: Place garlic in a bowl with pepper, salt and half the oil and mix gently. Add sugar and herbs, mix together again, add remaining oil and mix again. Finally, add the vinegar. Place in a screw top jar and shake several times. TO SERVE: Place several sardine fillets on hot finger toast or slices of fresh sourdough bread, top with the dressing, and garnish with parsley. *Serves four to six.*

Pacific Sardines Monterey Style

CHEF ROBERT MANCUSO, THE SARDINE FACTORY RESTAURANT, Monterey, California

✦

1½ pounds of fresh sardines, cleaned ▪ 6 sprigs fresh parsley, fried ▪ 2 lemons, quartered ▪ salt to taste ▪ BATTER MIX: ¾ cup flour ▪ 2 tablespoons olive oil ▪ 1 cup warm water ▪ 2 egg whites, beaten stiff ▪ ½ teaspoon salt ▪ 2 cups frying oil

Blend the batter. Add flour, oil, water, and salt. Fold egg whites into batter. Dip sardines into mixture, one by one, then dip them into 350°F frying oil. Drain on platter and sprinkle with salt.

TO SERVE: Place sardines on a plate and add chopped tomatoes, onions, and sprinkle with fried parsley. Use lemon as garnish. *Serves two to four.*

Sardines with Garlic and Balsamic Vinaigrette on Toasted Sourdough

Pacific Cod

Gadus macrocephalus

The Pacific cod is an important food source for the Steller's sea lion, an endangered and protected species. Fishing has been banned within 20 miles of the sea lion's habitat.

Cod is the king of whitefish, a species over which wars have been fought and from which trading fortunes have been made for hundreds of years. Today, two types of cod—Atlantic and Pacific—are as popular as ever. Their flaky white flesh has an almost universal appeal. Salt cod remains a staple food in Portugal, Spain, Italy, and Brazil, while fresh and frozen cod is widely consumed throughout North America, Europe, and Japan.

Found throughout the North Pacific, the Pacific cod is the world's second largest whitefish resource, exceeded only by Alaska pollock. The amount of cod caught in the Atlantic, however, is normally about four times that caught in the Pacific. A few East Coast fishermen maintain old-fashioned, sustainable fishing methods, where available, hook-and-line caught Atlantic cod is an eco-friendly choice. However, the Pacific cod is not overfished and therefore should be the cod of choice.

Seafood WATCH

Cod reproduce prolifically, and so should be able to sustain heavy fishing. But long-term overfishing and destruction of their seafloor habitat by bottom trawlers have sent Atlantic cod into drastic declines. A cousin, the Pacific cod, lives in the northern Pacific. Pacific cod are not overfished, and managers believe current harvest levels are sustainable. Until more data is obtained, Pacific cod is a "Good Alternatives."

For current fishery status, visit www.seafoodwatch.org

The Alaska fishery is by far the most important Pacific cod fishery. Alaska fishermen catch between 250,000 and 300,000 tons of Pacific cod each year using longline gear. The rest is caught by trawlers and pot boats.

Off the West Coast, where Pacific cod is often called "true cod," "gray cod," or "P-cod," less than 1,000 tons of cod are caught each year, primarily as a bycatch in the trawl fisheries for rockfish and flatfish. While almost all the West Coast cod catch is marketed as fresh fillets, the Alaska catch is almost all frozen, although some fresh cod fillets are air freighted from Alaska to markets in the "Lower 48" where cod is a favorite fish.

There can be significant quality differences with Pacific cod depending upon the time of the year the fish is caught. In the spring, for example, when cod are feeding heavily on small, oily fish like capelin, their flesh is noticeably softer. Quality is also a function of how the fish were handled. As a rule, the best fresh cod comes from short trips on boats that gut, bleed, and ice their fish.

Traditionally, Pacific cod was the fish of choice for fish sticks and fish sandwiches for fast-food restaurants. As cod prices increased, Alaska pollock replaced cod in these applications.

❖ ❖ ❖

Pacific cod is a mild-tasting fish, widely popular throughout North America. It can be used in a huge variety of preparations and is suitable for anything from "fish 'n' chip" stands to white tablecloth restaurants.

Sautéed Pacific Cod with Greek Walnut Salsa

Sautéed Pacific Cod with Greek Walnut Salsa

ALASKA SEAFOOD MARKETING INSTITUTE, Juneau, Alaska

◆

6 fresh Pacific cod fillets (6 ounces each) ▪ olive oil as needed ▪ FOR THE GREEK WALNUT SALSA: 1¼ cups tomatoes, finely chopped ▪ ½ cup cucumbers, finely chopped ▪ 2 tablespoons olives, finely chopped ▪ 2 tablespoons red onions, finely chopped ▪ 1 tablespoon lemon juice ▪ 1 teaspoon olive oil ▪ 1 teaspoon fresh parsley, chopped ▪ ¼ teaspoon garlic, minced ▪ pinch of dried oregano ▪ ¼ cup walnuts, chopped and toasted

Season cod fillets with salt and pepper. Sauté in oil in a sauté pan over medium-high heat until fish just flakes when tested with a fork. While fish is cooking, prepare the Greek Walnut Salsa by combining all ingredients except the walnuts until well combined.

Season with salt and pepper. Stir in walnuts just before serving. TO SERVE: Divide cod between serving plates and top evenly with salsa. *Serves six.*

Broiled Pacific Cod with Savory Rhubarb Sauce

WHOLE FOODS MARKET, Monterey, California

◆

4 fresh Pacific cod steaks (6 ounces each, about 1-inch thick) ▪ 2 teaspoons organic extra virgin olive oil ▪ 2 shallots, minced (⅓ cup) ▪ 4 cups julienne rhubarb (from 1 pound rhubarb) ▪ 1 tablespoon sugar ▪ ¾ teaspoon salt ▪ ⅔ cup water ▪ 2 tablespoons fresh lemon juice ▪ 2 teaspoons Dijon mustard ▪ ¼ teaspoon pepper ▪ ⅓ cup chopped fresh dill ▪ 2 teaspoons unsalted butter

In a large nonstick skillet, heat oil over low heat. Add shallots and cook, stirring occasionally, for 5 minutes or until soft. Add rhubarb, sugar, and ¼ teaspoon of salt and cook 5 minutes, stirring frequently, until rhubarb is crisp-tender. Meanwhile, preheat broiler. Place Pacific cod on broiler pan and sprinkle with remaining ½ teaspoon salt. Broil cod 4 inches from heat for 4 minutes per side or until just cooked through. Transfer to 4 serving plates. Add water, lemon juice, mustard, and pepper to skillet with rhubarb. Bring to a boil. Remove pan from heat and add dill and butter, stirring until butter is creamy. TO SERVE: Spoon sauce over cod and serve immediately. *Serves four.*

Sablefish / Black Cod

Anoplopoma fimbria

The sablefish supports very lucrative fisheries in Alaska and British Columbia and is a smaller but valuable groundfish along the Washington, Oregon, and California coastline.

One of the market names for sablefish—"butterfish"—says it all. Exceptionally rich and flavorful, sablefish is the most expensive bottomfish landed by U.S. fishermen. Although more than 90 percent of the sablefish catch is exported to Japan, a growing number of chefs in the U.S. are learning to appreciate the buttery taste and texture of this fish.

Although sablefish are found on both sides of the North Pacific, the majority of the commercial catch comes from the eastern North Pacific, where sablefish are caught from the Bering Sea to central California. Although they are called black cod, sablefish do not belong to the cod family. They belong to the *Anoplopomatidae* family, a unique group of fish.

Along with Pacific halibut, sablefish are managed in Alaska and British Columbia by an IFQ (Individual Fishing Quota) system, which allows individual longline fishermen to harvest a predetermined amount of fish anytime during the March-to-November season.

The Canadian Sablefish Association reports that a reduced harvest ensures a healthy fish stock and a long-term future in the sablefish fishery. Independent catch monitoring, strict by-catch limits,

Seafood WATCH

Alaska and British Columbia
sablefish are "Best Choices"
because populations are abundant
and the fisheries are well managed.
Other West Coast fisheries are
struggling with overcapacity (too
many fishing boats) so these
sablefish earn a "Good Alternatives"
rating because management is
in disarray.

For current fishery status, visit
www.seafoodwatch.org

and a dedication to peer-reviewed science are only a few examples of how the precautionary approach to fisheries management is enshrined in every aspect of the British Columbia sablefish fishery.

Off the West Coast, longliners fish sablefish in the fall. Most of their catch is frozen and exported to Japan. Small amounts of sablefish are landed as bycatch year-round by West Coast draggers.

Those sablefish in Alaska are caught in deeper, colder water, and command a higher price as they have a higher oil content, firmer texture, and are much larger than those caught off the West Coast. As a result, Alaska produces about 75 percent of the 30,000–40,000 tons of sablefish caught off North America every year.

◆ ◆ ◆

Alaska and British Columbia sablefish are a best choice for seafood lovers because the populations are stable and the fisheries are well-managed.

Sablefish is a delicacy, and can be prepared either baked, sautéed, grilled, or broiled.

Porcini Dusted Sablefish over a Mussel Olive Oil Emulsion with Roasted Young Bell Peppers and Elephant Garlic

CHEF FREDERIC COUTON, THE CANNERY SEAFOOD HOUSE, Vancouver, Canada

❖

14-ounce sablefish fillet cut in half ▪ 8 ounces fresh mussels ▪ 8 ounces mini bell peppers ▪ 1 head elephant garlic (or regular garlic), peeled ▪ 1 cup fish stock ▪ 1 cup whipping cream ▪ ½ cup white wine ▪ 1 medium shallot, sliced ▪ 3 tablespoons extra virgin olive oil ▪ 2 tablespoons dried porcini mushrooms ▪ 1 teaspoon pesto ▪ 1 fresh thyme sprig ▪ 1 pinch of saffron ▪ sea salt and black pepper to taste ▪ 2 basil sprigs for garnish

Place the mushrooms in a pan and put them in an oven (250°F) for 45 minutes to make sure the mushrooms are completely dried. Let them cool to room temperature and place in a clean grinder (coffee grinder will do). Grind until they become a powder; reserve. Wash the peppers and dry with paper towel. Place the peppers and peeled garlic cloves in a bowl with pesto, 1 teaspoon olive oil, and a pinch of salt and pepper. Place on a roasting pan and put in hot oven (375°F) for 10 to 12 minutes until fork tender; reserve. In a pot over medium heat, pour ½ teaspoon olive oil and add the sliced shallots. Turn heat to low and sauté for 3 minutes until translucent. Add the saffron and mussels and stir all for one minute. Turn the heat to medium, pour the white wine over the mussels and place a lid over the pot. Cook for a couple of minutes until the mussels open. Remove the mussel meat and reserve (discard shells). Add the fish stock to the remaining liquid and reduce to half over medium heat (approx 4 minutes). Add the cream and reduce by half. Transfer the sauce through a sieve and into a blender, discarding the remaining solid. Emulsify the sauce for 30 seconds on high speed while slowly adding the remaining olive oil. Adjust seasoning and reserve. Place the sablefish on a plate, add seasoning and coat in the porcini powder. Place a nonstick sauté pan on medium heat with a drop of olive oil. Sear fish for 2 minutes on each side. Finish in a hot oven (375°F) for several minutes. Add the mussels to the sauce and warm. Warm the vegetables. Remove cooked sablefish and place on paper towel to absorb excess oil. TO SERVE: Place the fish on a serving dish with the vegetables. Finish with the sauce and basil sprigs. *Serves two.*

Porcini Dusted Sablefish over a Mussel Olive Oil Emulsion with Roasted Young Bell Peppers and Elephant Garlic

New Zealand Cod (Hoki)

Macruronus novaezelandiae

Hoki is New Zealand's most important commercial fish species. New Zealand's hoki fishery is managed by strict quotas, which allow only a set amount of hoki to be taken commercially each year.

Hoki is a deepwater fish, found at depths of 500-2,500 feet throughout the Southern Hemisphere, particularly in New Zealand and South Australian waters. It is blue-green in color, with silvery sides. They feed on small fish, squid, and crustaceans such as shrimp. Part of the *Hake* family, Hoki is also known as blue hake and blue grenadier.

A cod relative, hoki is New Zealand's most important commercial fish species, and is a major off-shore trawl fishery. Annual catches average between 200,000–240,000 tons. Hoki has been New Zealand's biggest single fish export for a number of years. Recent years have seen a significant increase

Seafood WATCH

The New Zealand hoki fishery was recently certified sustainable by the Marine Stewardship Council (MSC), earning the fish a "Best Choice" rating. The MSC is an independent certification program that explores the fishery from ocean to table. The MSC is, however, still tracking concerns with bycatch of fur seals in this fishery.

For current fishery status, visit www.seafoodwatch.org

in earnings as the hoki industry has improved its processing methods and produced higher value products. The United States is the main market for hoki exports, followed by Japan.

Hoki is fished by mid-water and bottom trawling. Despite declining stocks and the continued take of fur seals and seabirds, the New Zealand hoki fishery certified the species sustainable by the Marine Stewardship Council, an independent body that analyzed the Hoki fishery.

Hoki is fished all year round, but the main fishing season runs for around 10 weeks between June and September. This is when hoki spawn, and is the only time they aggregate (come together) and so are easier to catch.

Because hoki produce so many eggs, targeting spawning fish may not be too harmful to the future of the fishery if the fishing effort is carefully controlled. The hoki spawning grounds are mostly inside a limited fishing zone that excludes larger vessels and offers some protection to spawning fish.

✦ ✦ ✦

Hoki is now an internationally-accepted white fish with the majority used for prime white fish portions and ready-to-cook battered and breaded fish products, particularly fish-and-chips. Hoki has a delicate, white, moist flesh with few bones. Because the skin is very soft, free of scales, and mild flavored, fillets are sold and consumed both with the skin on and the skin off.

Serrano Ham-Wrapped Roasted Red Hoki with Asopao Sauce and Olive-Oil Mâche-Radish Salad over Rice

Serrano Ham-Wrapped Roasted Red Hoki with Asopao Sauce and Olive-Oil Mâche-Radish Salad over Rice

Chef Jeff Jake, The Lodge at Pebble Beach, Pebble Beach, California

◆

6 New Zealand hoki fillets (4 ounces each) ▪ 12 thin slices serrano or prosciutto ham ▪ 4 tablespoons lemon oil ▪ 1 tablespoon sherry vinegar ▪ 2 tablespoons fresh thyme leaves ▪ 2 tablespoons vegetable oil ▪ Spanish rice ▪ **For the Sofrito:** 1 tablespoon vegetable oil ▪ 1 small onion, diced ▪ 1 small green bell pepper, seeded ▪ 3 aji dulce peppers or 1 to 2 small red and yellow bell peppers, diced ▪ ¼ cup cilantro ▪ 2 cloves garlic ▪ 2 tablespoons olive oil ▪ **For the sauce:** 1 small tomato, diced ▪ 1½ teaspoons capers ▪ ½ cup tomato sauce ▪ 3 cups water ▪ **For the Mâche-radish salad:** 1 cup Mâche leaves ▪ 3 tablespoons lemon oil ▪ 2 radishes, sliced into thin coins ▪ salt and pepper to taste

Marinate hoki with lemon oil, thyme, and vinegar for 3 hours in refrigerator. Turn hoki over every half-hour. Remove hoki from marinade and lightly salt and pepper. Be careful not to over salt the fish, since the ham is slightly salty. Wrap hoki in serrano or proscuttio ham across center of each fillet and reserve. Heat vegetable oil over medium heat in a sauté pan. When oil is hot, sauté hoki for 2 to 3 minutes on each side, then place the sauté pan in a preheated 350°F oven for approximately 8 minutes, depending on the thickness of the hoki fillets. **For the Sofrito:** In a medium saucepan, make Sofrito. Heat vegetable oil over medium heat, add diced onions, peppers, and herbs. Cook over medium heat, add olive oil and mix thoroughly. **For the sauce:** Add tomato, capers, and tomato sauce to Sofrito ingredients and bring to a boil. Add water and stir to combine all ingredients. Turn up heat and return to a boil, stirring well. Lower heat and allow sauce to simmer for 15 minutes until it reaches desired consistency. **For the Mâche-radish salad:** Gently toss ingredients together and adjust seasoning. **To serve:** Place a large spoonful of Spanish rice (cook according to package directions) in the center of a large, shallow serving bowl. Place hoki fillet on top of rice and spoon the Asopao sauce over fish. Top with the Mâche-Radish Salad and serve. *Serves six.*

Dover Sole

Microstomus pacificus

The majority of the dover sole population inhabits deep waters between 1,500 and 4,500 feet. They are also one of the longest living flatfish with a maximum lifespan of 60 years.

True soles belong to the *Soleidae* family. The highest value sole, the true Dover sole, *Solea solea*, is fished in the eastern North Atlantic off Europe. Small quantities of true Dover are exported to white tablecloth restaurants in the United States, primarily on the East Coast.

The popular "dover sole" fished off the West Coast and Alaska, *Microstomus pacificus*, is actually a flounder, and sells for considerably less than its European namesake. It lives at depths of 600 fathoms (3,600 feet) from northern Baja, California, to the Bering Sea. This "dover sole" is relatively long-lived, normally reaching 40 to 60 years. Common foods include mollusks, sea worms, shrimp, and brittle stars. Although these dover soles can reach ten pounds in size, most are one to one-and-one-half pounds and fillets average two to four ounces.

The West Coast dover sole is a popular flatfish you'll find marketed by your grocer or restaurant as "sole" in the United States. These dover sole are taken commercially in state and federal waters off California, Oregon, and Washington. Dover are also commercially trawled off the coast of Canada, which is the second largest exporter of soles to the United States.

Western dover sole live in the Pacific Ocean where populations are healthy, but their method of catch—bottom trawling—can impact the seafloor habitat. Generally, bottom trawling on sandy or

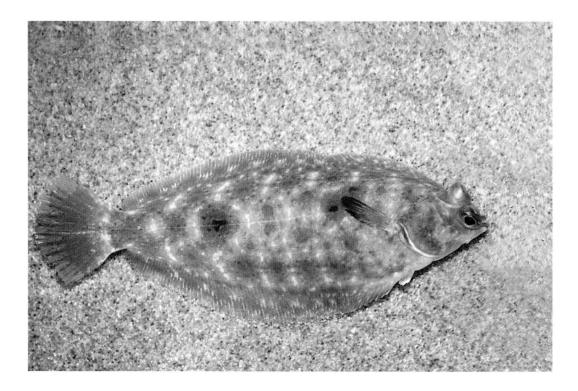

muddy seafloor where flatfish live is less damaging than trawling over rocky habitats. However, due to the potential habitat damage caused by such bottom-fishing methods, Pacific soles, including the West Coast dover sole, should be purchased with caution.

✦ ✦ ✦

The excellent quality of the flesh and its good keeping qualities in frozen storage have made dover sole one of the more important fishes in the flatfish category on the Pacific coast.

The flesh of the dover sole ranges in color from cream to white and has a delicate texture. However, some fillets are excessively milky or gelatinous. These are commonly called "Deep Water Dover," even though they may not have been caught in deep water.

Many of the dover sole landed along the west coast are delivered fresh to market, but in fishing areas far from population centers (such as Alaska), the sole are put in a block and frozen whole. Another common process is to remove the head and tail, leave in the guts (called kirimi), and then freeze the fish. Flatfish are difficult to fillet by hand, so that stage of the process usually waits until the fish gets to the retailer or restaurant.

Fillet of Dover Sole in Artichoke Bottoms

CHEF JACQUES PEPIN, *from the Book* JACQUES PEPIN'S KITCHEN: ENCORE WITH CLAUDINE

◆

FOR THE ARTICHOKES: 4 artichokes ▪ 1 tablespoon lemon juice ▪ 1 cup water ▪ ¼ teaspoon salt ▪ FOR THE MUSHROOM DUXELLES: 3 tablespoons shallots, peeled and finely chopped ▪ 1 tablespoon virgin olive oil ▪ 6 ounces cremini mushrooms, washed and coarsely chopped ▪ ¼ teaspoon salt ▪ ¼ teaspoon freshly-ground black pepper ▪ FOR THE SOLE: 1 pound fresh dover sole fillets (4 fillets) ▪ 1 large ripe tomato (8 ounces), cut into 1-inch pieces ▪ ¼ teaspoon salt ▪ ¼ teaspoon freshly-ground black pepper ▪ ¼ cup fruity dry white wine (like a Sauvignon blanc) ▪ 2 tablespoons virgin olive oil ▪ 1 tablespoon fresh parsley, chopped

FOR THE ARTICHOKES: Remove the stems from the artichokes, cutting them off at the base. Remove all the petals of each artichoke so just the bottom remains. Place the bottoms in a saucepan with the stems, and add the lemon juice, water, and the ¼ teaspoon salt. Bring the mixture to a boil, cover, reduce the heat to low, and cook gently for 18 to 20 minutes, until the artichoke bottoms and stems are tender. Using a slotted spoon, transfer the bottoms and stems to a plate, and allow them to cool to lukewarm. When the artichoke bottoms are cool enough to handle, remove the chokes from each, forming a hole in the middle of the artichoke. Cut the stems lengthwise into 1-inch pieces or julienne them; set aside with the bottoms. Preheat the oven to 180°. FOR THE DUXELLES: Place the chopped shallots in a skillet with a tablespoon of olive oil, and cook for 2 minutes over medium heat. Add the chopped mushrooms and the ¼ teaspoon each salt and pepper. Sauté over medium to high heat for about 5 minutes, until the moisture from the mushrooms is gone and the mushrooms are lightly browned. Transfer the mushroom mixture to a 6-cup gratin dish, and arrange the artichoke bottoms on top and the stem pieces around them.

Keep warm in the 180° oven while you cook the sole. FOR THE SOLE: Fold in the ends of each fillet (as you would fold a letter) to create a somewhat square three-layered "package" and arrange the "packages" seam-side down in a skillet. Place the tomato pieces around the sole, and sprinkle the fish and the tomatoes with ¼ teaspoon each salt and pepper. Add the white wine. Bring the mixture to a boil over high heat, and boil for about 30 seconds. Then, turn the sole "packages" with a fork so they are seam-side up, cover, reduce the heat to medium, and cook for 2½ minutes. The fillets should be slightly undercooked in the center at this point. TO SERVE: Fill each artichoke bottom with the mushroom mixture. Arrange one sole fillet on top of each artichoke. Return the gratin dish to the 180° oven while you prepare the sauce. Place the cooking liquid with the tomato pieces in a measuring cup, and add the 2 tablespoons olive oil. Using a hand blender, emulsify the mixture for 30 to 40 seconds, until smooth and creamy. Pour the sauce over the sole fillets, and garnish with parsley and artichoke stems. Serve immediately. *Serves four.*

Fillet of Dover Sole in Artichoke Bottoms

Sanddabs

Citharichthys

The Pacific sanddab is one of the shortest living flatfish with a maximum lifespan of 10 years. In that short time frame, sanddabs grow rapidly in shallow nearshore areas.

In North America, three kinds of sanddabs live in the waters off California, but only two are commonly harvested for food—the Pacific sanddab *(Citharichthys sordidus)*, and the longfin sanddab *(Citharichthys xanthostigma)*. The third, the speckled sanddab, is so small (only about five inches) that it is only important to the diet of other marine fishes.

A member of the flatfish family, the Pacific sanddab can best be distinguished from the longfin sanddab by the length of the pectoral fin on the eyed side. It is always shorter than the head of the Pacific sanddab and longer than the head of the longfin. Sanddabs are always left "handed" (eyes on the left) and can be distinguished from all other left "handed" flatfish by having a midline that is nearly straight for its entire length.

The body of the Pacific sanddab is oblong. The head is deep; the eyes are on the left-side and are large. The color is light brown mottled with yellow and orange on the eyed side and white on the blind side. Conversely, the color of the longfin sanddab is dark brown with rust orange or white speckles, and the pectoral fin is black on the eyed side and white on the blind side.

Seafood WATCH

Sanddabs are caught by trawling on seafloor habitats. Although bottom trawling on sandy or muddy seafloor is less damaging to essential fish habitat than trawling over rocky habitat types, it does have some effect on habitat and has been shown to reduce species diversity. Other methods, such as seine and hook-and-line, are used by a small number of fishermen and have minimal impact to the seafloor. Most sanddabs in the market, however, come from commercial trawlers, so sanddabs are listed as a "Good Alternatives."

For current fishery status, visit www.seafoodwatch.org

Pacific saddabs range from Cape San Lucas in Baja, California, to the Bering Sea. They are most abundant at depths of 120 to 300 feet. Longfin sanddabs occur from Costa Rica to Monterey, California. These flatfish are usually found on sandy or muddy sea bottoms from eight to 660 feet.

Sanddabs, in general, eat a wide variety of food. In addition to such items as small fishes, squid, and octopus, they eat an assortment of eggs, luminescent sea squirts, shrimp, crabs, and marine worms.

Like the Western dover sole, sanddabs live in the Pacific Ocean where populations are healthy, but their method of catch—bottom trawling—can impact the seafloor habitat. Generally, bottom trawling on sandy or muddy seafloor where flatfish live is less damaging than trawling over rocky habitats. However, due to the potential habitat damage caused by such bottom-fishing methods, Pacific soles, including sanddabs, should be purchased with caution.

✦ ✦ ✦

Highly regarded as food, sanddabs are sought by anglers as well as commercial trawlers. They are harvested commercially by bottom fishermen using otter trawls. Although effective, bottom trawling can damage the sea floor and produce a fair amount of bycatch.

Roasted Sanddabs with Meyer Lemon Relish

Roasted Sanddabs with Meyer Lemon Relish

CHEF JEAN PIERRE MOULLÉ , CHEZ PANISSE, Berkley, California

✦

4 whole sanddabs, trimmed and cleaned ▪ salt and pepper as needed ▪ flour for dusting the fish ▪ ¼ cup extra virgin olive oil ▪ FOR THE MEYER LEMON RELISH: 1 large shallot, finely minced ▪ 1 tablespoon lemon juice ▪ 1 large Meyer lemon ▪ ½ cup extra virgin olive oil ▪ 2 tablespoons chopped parsley ▪ 1 tablespoon each of chopped chervil, chives and basil ▪ pinch of cayenne pepper ▪ salt to taste

Put the minced shallot in a bowl. Add the lemon juice and a pinch of salt. Macerate for 5 minutes. Cut the Meyer lemon into wedges. Remove the seeds and central core and cut into thin slivers. Combine the slivered lemon and shallot and stir in the olive oil, chopped herbs, and a pinch of cayenne pepper. Taste, adjust the seasoning and set aside at room temperature. Season the sanddabs with salt and pepper. Dust them lightly on both sides with flour. Heat a cast-iron skillet and add the olive oil. When the oil is hot, slip in the sanddabs and fry over medium heat for 1–2 minutes per side or until golden brown. Remove fish, place on paper towel, and cool to room temperature. TO SERVE: Arrange the sanddabs on a platter. Spread the Meyer lemon relish over the fish and serve immediately. *Serves two to four.*

VARIATION: *This dish works well with salmon, and many other fish.*

"Simmering Sanddabs" with Summer Vegetables and Pale Ale

CHEF JEFF MILLER, PAPOOSE CREEK LODGE, Cameron, Montana

✦

8 ounces fresh sanddab fillets ▪ 4 ounces sweet pork sausage, cut into 1-inch pieces ▪ 12–18 fresh black mussels, in shell ▪ 2 tablespoons olive oil ▪ ½ onion, julienne ▪ 1 bulb fennel, julienne ▪ 1 small leek, sliced in half lengthwise and sliced again in half-circle shape ▪ 6 cloves garlic, sliced ▪ 1 rib celery, sliced ▪ 1 teaspoon tomato paste ▪ 1 12-ounce bottle pale ale ▪ 1 cup water ▪ 2 ears sweet corn, cut in 2-inch cross sections (about 8 pieces) ▪ 1½ cups green beans, cut in 1-inch pieces ▪ 1½ cups potatoes cut in 1-inch dice ▪ 2 large tomatoes peeled, seeded, rough dice ▪ ¼ cup fresh parsley, chopped ▪ 2 tablespoons fresh chives and fresh basil, chopped ▪ salt and pepper to taste

Heat olive oil in an 8-quart, wide-bottom pot. Add sausage and cook until browned and almost cooked through. Remove the sausage, set aside, and add onion, fennel, leek, celery and garlic to the pot. Cook for a few minutes until translucent, then add the garlic and tomato paste. If pan appears to be too dry, add a little more olive oil and continue cooking for 2 minutes. Add the pale ale and water, bring to a boil, season with salt and pepper, then add the corn, green beans, and potatoes. Cover the pot with a lid and simmer for 5 minutes. Sprinkle salt and pepper over the fish fillets then add the sanddab fillets, diced tomatoes and browned sausage. Cover with a lid and cook until the mussels open (1 to 2 minutes). Taste the broth for salt and pepper, stir in fresh herbs. TO SERVE: Serve at the table, straight from the pot. Accompany with a hearty rustic baguette and cold pale ale. *Serves two to four.*

Petrale Sole

Eopsetta jordani

PETRALE SOLE

The state of Oregon claims the most landings of petrale sole along the U.S. West Coast, with California second, and Washington third. An insignificant volume is landed in Alaska.

The petrale sole is the most highly regarded flounder commonly caught off the West Coast. In the United States, there are three stocks regularly fished: a northern stock off Oregon and Washington, a central stock off northern California, and a southern stock off central California. Of the three states, Oregon claims the most landings per year.

A rather small resource, the total United States petrale landings are less than 5,000 tons a year, with the heaviest landings occurring when they school in late January.

Seafood WATCH

Despite a management plan intended to allow Pacific flatfish populations to rebuild, most stocks are still declining. Though new regulations appear to be effective, populations need time to reach healthy levels. For this reason, petrale sole is on the "Good Alternatives" list.

For current fishery status, visit www.seafoodwatch.org

Like the other Pacific flatfish, petrale sole are found on the West Coast. They range from the Bering Sea to Baja, California, from 50 to over 1,000-feet deep. Petrale feed on an assortment of small fish, shrimp, crabs, brittle stars, and marine worms.

Although petrale populations are healthy, their method of catch—bottom trawling—can impact the seafloor habitat. Generally, bottom trawling on sandy or muddy seafloor where flatfish live is less damaging than trawling over rocky habitats. Due to the potential habitat damage caused by such bottom-fishing methods, Pacific soles, including petrale, should be purchased with caution.

✦   ✦   ✦

Petrale average about two pounds in size and fillets typically run four to six ounces. Fresh petrale are sold whole or cleaned, skinned and headless as pan-ready, boneless fillets. Frozen sole is available whole and as boneless fillets as well.

Well-iced, fresh sole will last up to ten days. Well-glazed, frozen sole can last up to a year stored at -5 to -15°F.

Petrale Sole with Balsamic Butter Sauce

CHEF JOHN ASH, FETZER VINEYARDS, Hopeland, California

◆

1½ pounds fresh petrale sole fillets ▪ 2 tablespoons butter ▪ 2 tablespoons olive oil ▪ flour for dredging, preferably rice flour ▪ salt and pepper as needed ▪ FOR THE BALSAMIC BUTTER SAUCE: 1 tablespoon olive oil ▪ 2 teaspoons shallots, finely chopped ▪ ⅓ cup dry white wine or dry white vermouth ▪ 3 tablespoons white or golden balsamic vinegar ▪ ⅓ cup chicken or fish stock ▪ ⅓ cup heavy cream ▪ 3 to 4 tablespoons unsalted butter ▪ salt and pepper as needed

In a saucepan heat oil over moderate heat and add the shallots. Cook and stir for 1-2 minutes or until shallots soften but don't brown. Add the wine, vinegar, and stock, and turn up heat to moderately high and reduce by half, about 5 to 7 minutes. Add the cream and again reduce until sauce has thickened, 4 to 5 minutes. Stir occasionally during this time. Strain through a fine mesh strainer, add sauce back to pan and reduce heat to low. Whisk in the butter 1 tablespoon at a time. Sauce will thicken and take on a satiny sheen. Season to taste with salt and pepper. Keep warm until serving time. In a large sauté pan heat butter and oil over medium heat. Dredge sole fillets in the flour and sauté until golden on both sides. Season to taste with salt and pepper. TO SERVE: Place one sole fillet on a warm plate topped with the balsamic butter sauce. *Serves four.*

Petrale Sole with Sweet Onion, Heirloom Tomatoes and Thyme

CHEFS HELENE KENNAN & TERRI BUZZARD, THE GETTY CENTER, Los Angeles, California

◆

4 fresh petrale sole fillets (6-ounces each) ▪ 4 medium-size heirloom tomatoes of different color, diced ▪ 12 copollini or sweet pearl onions, peeled ▪ 2 large garlic cloves ▪ 3 teaspoons fresh thyme ▪ 7 tablespoons olive oil ▪ 1 cup chicken stock ▪ ½ cup dry white wine ▪ 2 pats unsalted butter

Coat onions lightly with olive oil and roast in 350°F oven until golden brown. Heat 3 tablespoons oil in heavy large skillet over medium heat. Add onions and garlic. Sauté until garlic is tender, about 2 minutes. Add chicken stock and wine; simmer 3 minutes. Add tomatoes and thyme. Simmer about 5 minutes. Add cold butter and stir until melted. Season to taste with salt and pepper. Keep warm. Season fish with salt and pepper. Heat remaining 3 tablespoons oil in another large skillet over medium-high heat. Add fish and sauté until golden and just opaque in center, about 3 minutes per side. TO SERVE: Divide tomato/onion mixture evenly into 4 shallow bowls, set fish on top in the middle of the bowl. Garnish with fresh thyme sprigs. *Serves four.*

Petrale Sole with Balsamic Butter Sauce

Pacific Halibut

Hippoglossus stenolepis

Halibut are the largest of all flatfish. Pacific halibut can grow to more than eight feet long and over 500 pounds, rightfully earning their Latin name, *Hippoglossus,* or "hippos of the sea." The largest ever recorded in the northern Pacific was a 495-pound fish caught near Petersburg, Alaska. However, most commercially caught halibut run 20 to 100 pounds. In general, large halibut (more than 80 to 100 pounds) are called "whales," while small ones (20 pounds or less) are known as "chicken halibut."

Pacific halibut are more elongated than most flatfishes, their width being about one-third their length. Small scales are imbedded in the skin. Both eyes are on their dark or upper side. The color on the dark side varies but tends to assume the coloration of the ocean bottom. The underside is lighter, appearing more like the water's surface from below. This color adaptation helps halibut avoid detection by both prey and predator.

Being strong swimmers, halibut are able to catch and feed on a large variety of fishes (cod, turbot, pollock) along with invertebrates such as crab and shrimp. Sometimes halibut leave the ocean bottom to feed on pelagic fish such as sand lance and herring.

Alaska and Canadian halibut are caught only by longline, which are quarter-mile "skates" of gear with baited hooks strung every five to ten feet. Ideally, the halibut are gaffed aboard alive, then bled, cleaned and iced. Alaska accounts for approximately 80 percent of the North American harvest of Pacific halibut. The annual quota now averages about 25,000 tons.

Fishing for Pacific halibut is regulated by the International Pacific Halibut Commission. Members from the United States and Canada meet yearly to review research, check the progress of the commercial fishery, and make regulations for the next fishing season. The management of halibut fishing by this Commission is intended to allow a maximum sustained yield of halibut.

✦　✦　✦

Pacific halibut are noted for their thick steaks and fillets, which boast a big flake, mild flavor and excellent versatility in the kitchen. Thanks to changes in the fishery's management, fresh halibut are now available eight months a year. Frozen product is available year-round.

Pacific Halibut with Morel Mushrooms, Green Asparagus and Truffled Yellow Split Pea Purée

Pacific Halibut with Morel Mushrooms, Green Asparagus and Truffled Yellow Split Pea Purée

CHEF FRANK PABST, BLUE WATER CAFÉ , Vancouver, Canada

◆

4 pieces (5 ounces each) of fresh halibut fillets (skinless) ▪ 20 pieces asparagus ▪ 250g of fresh morel mushrooms, cut in half ▪ ½ cup yellow split peas ▪ 3 shallots, thinly sliced ▪ 2 cloves garlic ▪ ½ carrot ▪ 1 sprig thyme ▪ 1 sprig parsley ▪ 1 tablespoon chopped parsley ▪ 2½ cups chicken bouillon ▪ 4 tablespoons unsalted butter ▪ 1 teaspoon black truffle oil ▪ 1 teaspoon freshly-squeezed lemon juice ▪ salt and pepper as needed ▪ extra virgin olive oil as needed

Cut off the asparagus tips (the first 2 inches) and cook in boiling salted water until just done. Cut the rest of the asparagus stems in smaller pieces and cook in the same water until they are well done. Cook 1 thinly-sliced shallot in some olive oil until translucent, add ½ cup chicken bouillon and cook until shallots are done. Put asparagus stems, shallots with bouillon and 1 tablespoon butter in a blender and mix until smooth, pass through strainer and season with salt (adjust consistency with some more bouillon if necessary, looking for a soup purée-like consistency). Cook yellow split peas with 1 thinly-sliced shallot, the ½ carrot, the garlic, thyme and rosemary, and 1½ cups of the chicken bouillon until well done and mushy (approx 35 minutes). Strain (keep any strained liquid), add 2 tablespoons butter, truffle oil and lemon juice. Remove herbs and discard. Mix everything in blender to a smooth thick purée (adjust consistency with strained liquid, check seasoning). Sauté cleaned morel mmushrooms in some olive oil and

1 tablespoon butter for 1 minute; season with salt and pepper, add 1 diced shallot, a touch of chopped garlic, and sauté for another minute. Add ½ cup chicken stock and simmer for a couple of minutes until the mushrooms are soft and tender. Add parsley and adjust seasoning with salt and pepper. Season the halibut fillets with salt and pepper and sear them in a hot pan in some olive oil until you have a nice golden crust; turn around carefully and finish in the oven at 400°F until just about done, depending on the thickness of fillets anywhere from 2 to 5 minutes (fish will continue cooking for a couple of minutes once it is taken out of the heat). TO SERVE: Put a dollop of the yellow split pea purée in the center of dish, align 5 hot asparagus spears on the purée and top them with the halibut fillet, making sure the tips can still be seen. Spoon the morel mushroom ragoût on the fish and any reduced mushroom bouillon around the plate. *Serves four.*

Sockeye Salmon

Oncorhynchus nerka

The U.S. market is flooded with inexpensive farmed salmon from Chile, Canada, and Norway. Salmon is also farmed to a limited extent in the United States. Raising salmon in net pens releases fish waste into the water and can spread disease and parasites to wild salmon.

In the wild salmon business, this is the money fish. More than three-quarters of the world sockeye harvest comes from Alaska and, in a good year, almost 80 percent of the value of that state's total salmon harvest consists of sockeye. Although most of the North American sockeye harvest is exported, there's a growing appetite for this great-tasting salmon in the Lower Forty-eight.

Sockeye salmon can be distinguished from Chinook, Coho, and pink salmon by their lack of large, black spots. Like other salmon, sockeye are anadromous: they live in the sea and enter freshwater systems to spawn. While in fresh water, juvenile sockeye salmon feed upon zooplankton and insects. In the ocean, sockeye continue to feed upon zooplankton, but will also prey upon small fishes and

occasionally squid. Sockeye grow quickly in the sea, usually reaching a size of four to eight pounds after one to four years. Mature sockeye salmon travel thousands of miles from ocean feeding areas to spawn in the same freshwater system where they were born. Like all Pacific salmon, sockeye salmon die within a few weeks after spawning.

The largest harvest of sockeye salmon in the world occurs in the Bristol Bay area of southwestern Alaska. As many as ten to more than 30 million sockeye salmon may be caught each year during a short, intensive fishery that lasts only a few weeks.

About 30 percent of the North American sockeye harvest is canned. Most of this product is exported to the United Kingdom and Australia, where canned salmon remains a popular item.

The quality of sockeye (and other wild salmon) will vary within the same run, depending upon when the fish are caught. Early in the run, fish will generally be brighter and have more oil as they have to migrate farther upriver. A higher percentage of fish caught late in the run will have darker skin and less oil, as these fish will not travel as far.

◆ ◆ ◆

The price of sockeye can vary for a number of reasons, including the method of capture. The most expensive sockeye are landed in a small troll fishery off the west coast of Vancouver Island (sockeye are not trolled in Alaska). Seine fish caught off Kodiak, Chignik, and Southeast Alaska are also premium quality and command a premium price. The least expensive sockeye are caught in Bristol Bay, where only gillnets can be fished.

Seafood WATCH

Wild-caught sockeye salmon from a well-managed fishery is the best environmental choice. Wild Alaska salmon was recently certified sustainable by the Marine Stewardship Council, earning Alaskan sockeye salmon a "Best Choice." Canned salmon can be farmed or wild-caught so check the label carefully before you buy.

For current fishery status, visit www.seafoodwatch.org

Saké Glazed Sockeye Salmon with Mizo Yuzu Vinaigrette, Sesame Spinach and Crispy Noodles

Chef Nora Pouillon, Restaurant Nora, Washington D.C.

◆

4 sockeye salmon fillets (4 to 5 ounces each) ▪ For the saké marinade: 4 tablespoons saké ▪ 4 tablespoons mirin (rice wine) ▪ 2 tablespoons sugar or less ▪ 4 ounces white miso ▪ For the vinaigrette (1 cup): 2 ounces white miso ▪ 3 tablespoons yuzu juice (available in Japanese groceries), or use lemon juice ▪ 1 tablespoon tamari or soy sauce ▪ 2 tablespoons ginger, chopped into 2-inch pieces ▪ 1 teaspoon ground black pepper ▪ 4 tablespoons water ▪ 6 to 8 tablespoons sunflower or safflower oil ▪ For the garnish: fresh bok choy ▪ carrots or red peppers as needed ▪ garlic, chopped as needed ▪ ginger as needed

Prepare the salmon by putting fish fillets in one layer in a flat-bottomed plastic or stainless steel pan. Cover with a moistened cheesecloth, pour marinade over it, and spread out to cover fish. Refrigerate over night (or at least 3 hours). Lift cheesecloth and residual marinade off the fish and discard. Heat oil in sauté pan, sear fish on glazed-side first until caramelized. Carefully turn fish and finish cooking other side in a preheated 450°F oven or leave in pan on medium heat for 3 to 4 minutes until cooked to desired doneness. Next, prepare the saké marinade by combining the saké, mirin and sugar in a saucepan and cook until alcohol is evaporated and sugar dissolved, about 2 to 3 minutes. Whisk in miso and cool. For the vinaigrette, purée miso, yuzu, tamari, ginger, pepper, and water in a blender. Slowly add oil to emulsify, reserve. In a wok, stir-fry bok choy, carrots or red peppers in sunflower oil with chopped garlic and ginger. Season with tamari and black pepper, or serve with stir-fried spinach seasoned with garlic, ginger, and sesame seeds. Next, fry fresh spaghettini (thin spaghetti). Tie 3 or 4 strands into a knot or a loose bow and fry in sunflower oil. To serve: Place stir-fried vegetables on a plate, top with caramelized fish and pour some vinaigrette around the vegetables. Top with crispy noodles and chives. *Serves four.*

Saké Glazed Sockeye Salmon with Mizo Yuzu Vinaigrette, Sesame Spinach and Crispy Noodles

Coho Salmon

Oncorhynchus kisutch

Alaska coho salmon have healthy and abundant populations along pristine habitats, including wood-lined and unobstructed freshwater streams.

Coho salmon, also called silver salmon, are found off the Pacific Coast, particularly in Washington, Canada, and Alaska.

Adult coho usually weigh eight to 12 pounds and are 24 to 30 inches long, but some weighing 31 pounds have been landed. Adults in saltwater or newly arrived in fresh water are bright silver with small black spots on the back and on the upper lobe of the caudal fin. They can be distinguished from Chinook salmon by the lack of black spots on the lower lobe of the tail and by their gray gums.

In North America, salmon fishermen catch about 25,000 tons of wild coho each year. The majority of this harvest comes from Alaska where coho are fished from July to September. About 40 percent of the North American coho harvest is caught by trollers, the preferred method of fishing compared to

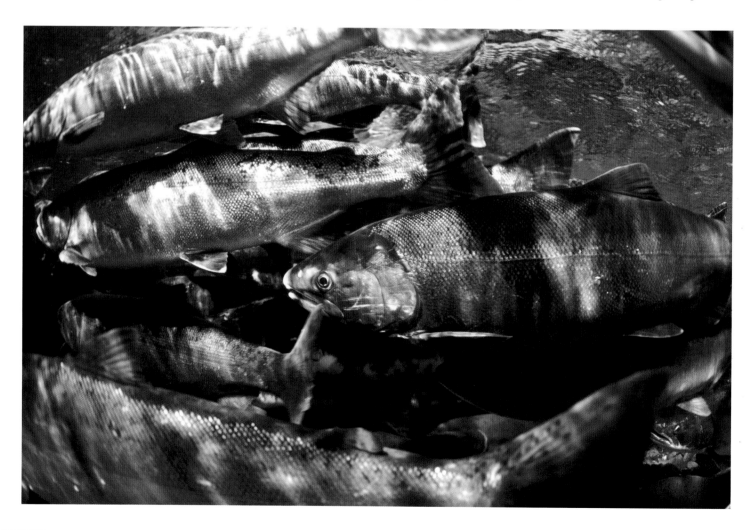

Seafood WATCH

Wild-caught coho salmon from a well-managed fishery is the best environmental choice. Wild Alaska salmon was recently certified sustainable by the Marine Stewardship Council, earning Alaskan coho salmon a "Best Choice." Canned salmon can be farmed or wild-caught so check the label carefully before you buy.

For current fishery status, visit www.seafoodwatch.org

nets. Troll-caught, frozen-at-sea (FAS) coho are considered the highest quality coho you can buy. Although not as highly regarded as king or sockeye, coho can be a great salmon for the money.

As a general rule, the bigger the salmon, the higher the yield—and the higher the price. But that's not always the case with coho. The market places a premium on four to six-pound fish because they are the ideal size for supermarkets. As a result, larger coho sell for a slight discount.

Some wild coho runs have a reputation for producing softer-fleshed fish than other runs. However, the softness is a function of how well the fish was handled—not the waters from which it came. The fishermen in some remote fisheries in Alaska do not always bleed and ice their fish, which results in softer fish.

✦   ✦   ✦

Coho salmon have a bright red color flesh—similar to that of sockeye salmon. Though the oil content is lower than sockeye or kings, coho salmon still boast a high oil content relative to other species of fish, which makes them excellent grilled, baked or broiled.

Coho Salmon with Pistachio, Basil and Mint Butter

Coho Salmon with Pistachio, Basil and Mint Butter

Chef Karen Barnaby, The Fish House in Stanley Park, Vancouver, Canada

◆

6 salmon fillets (6 ounces each) ▪ ¼ cup shelled pistachios ▪ ¼ cup fresh basil leaves ▪ ¼ cup fresh mint leaves
▪ 1 clove garlic, minced ▪ ½ cup unsalted butter, room temperature ▪ 1 tablespoon lemon juice ▪ ½ cup dry white
wine ▪ salt and pepper to taste

Pulse pistachios, basil, mint, and garlic in food processor until coarsely chopped. Add the butter and lemon juice and season to taste. Pulse until everything is smoothly mixed. Transfer to a small bowl and refrigerate until cold. The butter can be prepared up to 4 days in advance. Preheat the oven to 400°F. Butter a 9x13 inch baking dish and lay out the salmon fillets in a single layer. Pour the wine over the salmon and season to taste. Bake salmon until almost opaque on top, about 10 minutes. Place 2 tablespoons of the butter on top of each salmon piece. Continue baking until the salmon is just opaque in the center, about 5 minutes. Transfer to plates and pour the baking juices from the pan over top. *Serves six.*

Wild Coho Salmon with Citrus Peppercorn Sauce

Chef Paul Buchanan, Primal Alchemy, Long Beach, California

◆

4 portions of fresh coho salmon (6-ounces each, skin off, pin bone out) ▪ olive oil, as needed ▪ kosher salt and
ground white pepper to taste ▪ FOR THE SAUCE: 2 fresh lemons ▪ 2 fresh limes ▪ 3 fresh oranges ▪ 2 tablespoons rice
wine vinegar ▪ 1 teaspoon natural raw granulated sugar ▪ kosher salt and ground white pepper to taste

FOR THE SAUCE: Using a zester, take the outer skin of the 3 types of citrus into a small pan, fill with cold water and bring to a boil; immediately remove from the heat, drain and rinse the zest in cold water. Repeat this boiling process 1-2 more times. This removes all wax and impurities from the skin and makes the zest more edible. Now take a chef's knife and remove all the skin and white pith that is left on each citrus so that only the meat of each citrus shows. Using the same sharp knife, carefully remove the segments of citrus by slicing a wedge shape between each white segment separation. Lastly, squeeze the remaining juice in each citrus and reserve. Combine all of the ingredients, except for the salmon, into a large bowl. Adjust sugar, vinegar, salt and pepper to taste; set aside. FOR THE FISH: Take a dry sauté pan or cast iron skillet and place it over a high flame for 4-5 minutes until hot. Season the salmon portions with kosher salt and white pepper on both sides. When pan is hot, place approximately 1½ tablespoons of olive oil into the pan and immediately add the salmon fillets; do not move them for about 2 minutes, cook until dark golden brown. Turn over the fillet and cook to medium rare. TO SERVE: Place salmon on plate, spoon the citrus sauce over, and accompany with fresh steamed organic garden vegetables and wild rice. *Serves four.*

Chinook Salmon

Oncorhynchus tschawytscha

The chinook or "king" salmon is Alaska's state fish and is one of the most important sport and commercial fish species in the Pacific coast waters of North America. It is the largest of all Pacific salmon, commonly exceeding 30 pounds. The record is held by a 126-pound chinook salmon that was taken in a fish trap near Petersburg, Alaska, in 1949. The largest sport-caught chinook salmon was a 97-pound fish taken in the Kenai River in 1986.

Adult chinook salmon are distinguished by the black, irregular spotting on the back and dorsal fins and on both lobes of the caudal or tail fin. Chinook salmon also have a black pigment along the gum line which causes them to be called "blackmouth" in some areas.

In the ocean, the chinook salmon is a robust, deep-bodied fish with a bluish-green coloration on the back, which turns to a silvery color on the sides and white on the belly. Colors of spawning chinook salmon in fresh water range from red to copper to almost black, depending on location and maturity.

Like all species of Pacific salmon, chinook salmon are anadromous. They hatch in fresh water, spend part of their life in the ocean, and then spawn in fresh water. Juvenile chinooks in fresh water feed on plankton, then later eat insects. In the ocean, they eat a variety of organisms including herring, pilchard, sandlance, squid, and crustaceans. Salmon grow rapidly in the ocean and often double their weight during a single summer season. A mature three-year-old will probably weigh less than four pounds, while a mature seven-year-old may exceed 50 pounds. All chinooks die shortly after spawning.

Unlike other salmon species, chinook salmon mature in inshore marine waters and are, therefore, available to commercial and sport fishermen all year. Catches of chinook salmon in Southeast Alaska are regulated by quotas set under the Pacific Salmon Treaty. In other regions of Alaska, chinook salmon fisheries are also closely managed to ensure stocks are not over-harvested.

✦ ✦ ✦

King salmon have the highest oil content of all five species of wild salmon. They are often smoked because the fat content helps the flesh retain its characteristic moistness. This much-loved fish is excellent prepared in almost any way, though simple, unobtrusive methods are perfect for letting the natural flavor of the king shine through.

Seafood WATCH

Wild-caught chinook (king) salmon from a well-managed fishery is the best environmental choice. Wild Alaska salmon was recently certified sustainable by the Marine Stewardship Council, earning Alaskan Chinook salmon a "Best Choice." Canned salmon can be farmed or wild-caught so check the label carefully before you buy.

For current fishery status, visit www.seafoodwatch.org

"Sashimi" Grilled Copper River King Salmon with Wasabi Aïoli, Soy-Maple Drizzle

CHEF STEVE GADBOIS, Vancouver, Canada

✦

1 pound salmon ■ FOR THE "SASHIMI" MARINADE: 3 tablespoons sesame oil ■ 1 cup ginger root, peeled and grated ■ ¼ cup garlic cloves, crushed ■ 1½ cups soy sauce or tamari ■ 3 cups water ■ 1 cup rice wine ■ FOR THE WASABI AÏOLI: 1 cup mayonnaise ■ 1½ tablespoons fresh lemon juice ■ ¼ teaspoon kosher salt ■ 1 teaspoon minced garlic ■ 2 teaspoons minced ginger ■ ⅛ cup wasabi powder ■ ACCOMPANIMENT: 4 heads baby bok choy, cut in half ■ 1 package daikon sprouts ■ ⅛ cup sushi ginger for garnish ■ SOY-MAPLE REDUCTION: ½ cup maple syrup, grade A ■ ¼ cup soy sauce

FOR THE SASHIMI marinade: In a small saucepan heat the sesame oil under medium heat and sweat the garlic and ginger until soft. Deglaze with the rice wine and reduce for 30 seconds. Next add the water, soy and bring to just a boil. Remove from heat and cool. When cool, add the salmon fillets to the marinade and refrigerate for 2 hours. SOY-MAPLE REDUCTION: Combine maple syrup and soy sauce in a small saucepan over medium heat and reduce to about ⅔ cup. WASABI AÏOLI: Combine garlic, mayonnaise, ginger, salt, and lemon juice in a food processor. Blend at high speed until combined. Mix wasabi powder with enough water to make a thick paste. Fold wasabi into the aïoli until blended. SERVICE: Remove the salmon from the marinade and pat dry. Oil the fillets and grill over high heat for 2 to 3 minutes on each side. Slice the baby bok choy in half and grill until caramelized. Remove from grill and rest in a warm place. TO SERVE: Drizzle the soy maple around the plate. Lay the bok choy near the center. Lay the salmon on the vegetables and top with a dollop of aïoli, sushi ginger and daikon sprouts. *Serves four.*

Baked King Salmon with Smoked Salmon Horseradish Crust and Beurre Blanc

CHEF JAMISON BRANDT, LAKE CRESCENT LODGE, Port Angeles, Washington

✦

SALMON AND SMOKED SALMON HORSERADISH CRUST: 2 fresh king salmon fillet pieces (6 ounces each, pin bones out) ■ 1 piece wild smoked salmon (6-ounces) ■ ½ cup freshly-shredded horseradish root ■ 1 cup sliced scallions (⅛ inch-thick) ■ ½ cup bread crumbs ■ BEURRE BLANC: 1 teaspoon minced shallots ■ ½ lemon (juiced) ■ one pinch each salt and pepper ■ ¼ cup white wine ■ 3 ounces unsalted butter (room temp) ■ SWEET POTATO POMMES FRITES: 1 large sweet potato peeled and halved into ⅛-inch julienne slices ■ fresh spring asparagus and chives for garnish

FOR SMOKED SALMON HORSERADISH CRUST: Combine smoked salmon, bread crumbs, and pepper, and chop in food processor (not too fine). Place into a mixing bowl and add shredded horseradish root and scallions. Mix together. Place the two 6-ounce king salmon fillets on baking sheet. Add a thick layer of smoked salmon crust on top and place in oven at 400°F until salmon is medium-rare to medium in temperature. Put sweet potato frites in 350°F fryer until golden brown. In a sauce pan, sweat shallots with salt and pepper. Add white wine and lemon juice on high heat, and reduce by three-quarters. Turn off heat, add butter and mix together. TO SERVE: Divide the frites in the center of 2 plates, and top with the king salmon fillets. Ladle the buerre blanc around salmon and frites and garnish with spring asparagus and chives. *Serves two.*

"Sashimi" Grilled Copper River King Salmon with Wasabi Aïoli, Soy-Maple Drizzle

Spanish Mackerel

Scomberomorus maculatus

SPANISH MACKEREL

Spanish mackerel are managed in both federal and state waters of the Atlantic and Gulf of Mexico. Current commercial fishery management measures include size limits, total allowable catch, trip limits, gear restrictions, and permit requirements.

In the southeastern United States, mackerel is a popular catch in both recreational and commercial fisheries. The two species most commonly caught in this region are king and Spanish mackerel. There is one population of Spanish mackerel, which is managed as two groups in the Gulf of Mexico and South Atlantic.

Spanish mackerel are coastal pelagic finfish. They prefer open water but are sometimes found over deep grass beds and reefs, as well as in shallow water estuaries. Spanish mackerel form large, fast-moving schools that migrate great distances along the shore. They feed on small fishes, squid and shrimp, often forcing schools of prey into crowded clumps and practically pushing the fish out of the water as they feed. Spanish mackerel grow to 37 inches and average two to three pounds. Fish older than five years are rare, though some females have been known to reach 11 years.

The slender, elongated body of the Spanish mackerel is silvery on the underside with a bluish or olive-green back. Their distinguishing marks are the many small yellow and olive spots above and below the lateral line on both sides.

Seafood WATCH

Since a ban on gillnets in Florida in 1995 was put in place, fishermen in the Gulf of Mexico have taken Spanish mackerel using hook-and-line gear, greatly reducing their catch. Because of these restrictions, Spanish mackerel are abundant in the Gulf of Mexico as well as the Atlantic, where they are caught predominately by trolling, another gear with low bycatch. For these reasons Spanish mackerel is a "Best Choice."

For current fishery status, visit www.seafoodwatch.org

Spanish mackerel mature quickly and spawn prolifically, making them resilient to fishing pressure. However, juvenile Spanish mackerel are frequently caught as bycatch in the Gulf shrimp trawl fishery. Since a ban on gillnets in Florida state waters in 1995 was put in place, these fishermen have taken Spanish mackerel using hook-and-line gear, greatly reducing their catch. Because of these restrictions, Spanish mackerel are abundant in the Gulf of Mexico and those from Florida should be requested.

❖ ❖ ❖

Spanish mackerel are available fresh or frozen, whole, dressed, filleted or as steaks. They are an excellent food fish—comparable to king mackerel, tuna and mullet—with moderate texture and full flavor. Although suitable for frying, they are best broiled, baked or smoked.

Spanish Mackerel with Lemon, Celery and Thyme

Spanish Mackerel with Lemon, Celery and Thyme

CHEF GORDON HAMERSLEY, HAMERSLEY'S BISTRO, Boston, Massachusetts

✦

4 fresh fillets of Spanish mackerel (6 ounces each) with skin removed ▪ 2 shallots, peeled and thinly sliced ▪ 12 leaves from the tops of celery ▪ 2 teaspoons thyme ▪ red pepper flakes as needed ▪ 1 lemon, cut into 4 thin slices ▪ ½ cup white wine ▪ ½ cup extra virgin olive oil ▪ sea salt and black pepper to taste

Preheat the oven to 350°F. Cut 4 pieces of aluminum foil large enough to hold the mackerel fillets with about 4 inches extra all around so the fish can be enclosed in the foil. Place each fillet in the center of each piece of foil. Season with salt and pepper. Evenly add the sliced shallot on top of each fillet, the celery leaves, thyme, red pepper flakes, and lemon slices. Add the white wine and olive oil. Fold the sides of the foil up and bind it together to form a sealed pouch. Place the foil pouches on a sheet pan and place into the oven. Cook for about 7 to 9 minutes depending on how thick the fish, until just cooked. Remove the foil pouches from the oven. TO SERVE: Transfer the foil pouches to 4 plates. Let each diner unwrap their pouch and slide the contents onto their plate. Serve with steamed potatoes or rice. *Serves four.*

Baked Spanish Mackerel with Butter, Lemon and Paprika

BUREAU OF SEAFOOD & AGRICULTURE, Tallahassee, Florida

✦

2 pounds fresh Spanish mackerel fillets ▪ 1 teaspoon sea salt ▪ ⅛ teaspoon black pepper ▪ ¼ cup unsalted butter, melted ▪ 2 tablespoons fresh lemon juice ▪ 1 teaspoon grated onion ▪ ⅛ teaspoon paprika ▪ lemon wedges for garnish

Sprinkle fillets with salt and pepper. Place in a single layer on a well-oiled baking pan. Combine butter, lemon juice and paprika. Cover fillets with the sauce. Bake at 350°F for about 20 minutes, or until fish flakes easily when tested with a fork. TO SERVE: Place 1 or 2 Spanish mackerel fillets on a plate and garnish with lemon wedges. *Serves six.*

White Sea Bass

Atractoscion nobilis

In the commercial fishery, the white sea bass catch has steadily increased since the 1990s. Recent information about the wild stock indicates the population off California is recovering.

Found in all tropical and warm seas, sea bass come in over 30 genera with over 500 species. The white sea bass, however, is actually not a true bass but instead is the largest member of the croaker family (sometimes called "king croaker"). They inhabit the waters off the Pacific coast from California to Mexico. Prized for their large size and high food quality, white sea bass have been fished both commercially and for sport since the early 1900s.

The white sea bass has an elongated body, which is blue-gray above with fine black speckling. The underneath is silvery. Its head is small compared to the rest of its body, with a lower jaw slightly longer than the upper.

Despite their small eyes, white sea bass are tremendous predators, feeding on squid, pelagic red crabs, anchovies, sardines, and other small fish. White sea bass can reach five feet and 90 pounds, although the average length is about three feet and they are rarely found weighing more than 60 pounds. Like other croakers, the male white sea bass emits a characteristic "croaking" sound, produced by vibrating its air bladder.

White sea bass live in different habitats at different life stages. Very young sea bass from two to four inches live in drift algae just behind the surf line. Older juveniles occupy bays and shallow coastal waters. Adults are usually found near reefs or kelp beds. Large adults move into deeper water (120–350 feet) during the winter. The current center of the white sea bass population appears to be located off central Baja, California.

Commercially, white sea bass are caught off the California coast primarily using hook-and-line. The commercial white sea bass fishery is relatively small; over the last 20 years there has been an average of 140 vessels in the fleet. This allows the white sea bass to reproduce and populate, maintaining a healthy stock. With new management efforts, including supplementing the wild population with hatchery-raised fish, California's white sea bass population is very abundant.

✦ ✦ ✦

White sea bass are very important to seafood restaurants on the west coast, particularly in California, where it is often found on menus. White sea bass flesh is pure white and very light tasting. Larger fillets are ideal for barbecuing.

Crab Crusted White Sea Bass with Green Onion Mashed Potatoes, Fresh Asparagus and Sweet Red Pepper Sauce

PHILLIPS FOODS, INC., Baltimore, Maryland

✦

6 white sea bass fillets (6 ounces each) ▪ 1 pound lump crab meat, picked and cleaned ▪ 1 tablespoon seafood seasoning ▪ 8 ounces cream cheese ▪ ½ cup mayonnaise ▪ 1 tablespoon Dijon mustard ▪ 1 tablespoon powdered sugar ▪ 1 teaspoon onion juice ▪ ½ cup sherry wine ▪ salt and white pepper to taste ▪ SWEET RED PEPPER SAUCE: 1 cup roasted red peppers ▪ 2 tablespoons olive oil ▪ 1 teaspoon garlic, chopped ▪ 1 tablespoon parsley ▪ ¼ cup sautéed onions ▪ mashed potatoes with sliced green onions (as needed)

Preheat oven to 375°F. FOR THE CRAB CRUST: Combine the cream cheese, mayonnaise, mustard, powdered sugar, onion juice, and seafood seasoning. Adjust ingredients to taste. Place the combined ingredients in a stainless steel bowl over a double boiler and mix until smooth and creamy. Add the sherry, and salt and pepper to taste. Blend well and remove from heat. After the mixture has cooled, fold in the lump crab meat. Season the white sea bass with salt and pepper and spread a liberal layer of the crab mixture evenly on top of each fillet. Bake on buttered parchment paper at 375°F for about 15 minutes (or until crust is golden brown and the fish is cooked through). Watch carefully; do not overcook. While fish is cooking, prepare the Sweet Red Pepper Sauce by combining the ingredients in a food processor. Puree until smooth. TO SERVE: Place the sea bass on top of green onion mashed potatoes with a side of asparagus in sweet red pepper sauce. *Serves six.*

Seared White Sea Bass over Grilled Vegetable Ragoût with White Truffle Oil and Fish Bordelaise

CHEF TERRY TEPLITZKY, MICHAEL'S CATERING / WILD THYME DELICATESSEN, Marina, California

✦

4 fresh bass fillets (6-ounces each, skin on) ▪ 3 tablespoons olive oil ▪ salt and pepper to taste ▪ BORDELAISE SAUCE: 1 shallot, finely chopped ▪ ¼ cup white wine ▪ 4 tablespoons cream ▪ ¾ pound butter, cut into cubes ▪ 2 tablespoons fresh chives ▪ salt and pepper to taste ▪ whole chives for garnish ▪ VEGETABLES: 16 fresh asparagus spears, trim off bottom and cut down 3-inch tips ▪ 4 portabella mushrooms, de-stemmed ▪ 2 medium heads of radicchio, cut into ½" pieces ▪ salt and pepper to taste ▪ olive oil and white truffle oil as needed

Coat vegetables with oil, salt and pepper, and grill lightly. Be careful not to over-char. Cool and cut into julienne slices. Keep warm. Heat 2 tablespoons olive oil in large sauté pan. Salt and pepper and spray fish fillets with nonstick spray. When oil smokes, sear fish, flesh side down, in hot oil for 3 minutes. Turn and cook for 3 more minutes. Skin should be crispy. Place fish fillets on plate in warm oven. Quickly add shallots to the hot pan and deglaze with white wine. Reduce liquid by half. Add cream until thickened. Add butter and swirl pan. When butter has incorporated, add salt, pepper and chives. TO SERVE: Mound ¼ of grilled vegetables on each bowl or plate. Place fish fillet on top, skin side up. Pour ¼ of sauce over fish and around bowl. Sprinkle with truffle oil and garnish with chives. *Serves four.*

Crab Crusted White Sea Bass with Green Onion Mashed Potatoes, Fresh Asparagus and Sweet Red Pepper Sauce

Striped Bass

Morone saxatilis

Farm raised striped bass are placed in specially prepared ponds, cages, tanks or raceways filled with high-quality water. The bass are fed a balanced specially-prepared diet that allows them to grow to market size—one to three pounds—in less than two years.

The striped bass is the largest member of the sea bass family. It is a silvery fish that gets its name from the seven or eight dark, continuous stripes along the side of its body. Mature stripers are known for their fighting ability and size—they've been known to reach 100 pounds and nearly five feet in length. The farmed variety is actually a cross between the striped bass and the white bass, and is slightly stubbier with a broken striped pattern.

Striped bass are anadromous fish (normally living in saltwater, but entering freshwater streams to spawn), and have been widely introduced in numerous lakes, rivers, shores, bays, and estuaries

throughout the world. In North America, striped bass are native to the Atlantic coast from St. Lawrence River, Canada, to St. Johns River, Florida, although they are most prevalent from Maine to North Carolina.

Stripers are voracious feeders and consume any kind of small fish and a variety of invertebrates. Preferred foods for adults consist of shad, golden shiners and minnows. Striped bass are fast-growing and relatively long-lived. A male is mature at age three and 18 inches long. In favorable conditions, wild striped bass can live more than 30 years.

About half the striped bass sold in markets today are produced by aquaculture, relieving the pressure on wild stocks. They are farmed inland using closed, non-polluting systems. Wild striped bass are caught commercially with hook and line as well as gillnets which entail moderate bycatch. Hook and line caught stripers are the best choice when choosing wild striped bass.

Thanks to fishery projects such as the Chesapeake Bay Striped Bass Fishery Management Plan and the Fishery Management Plan for the Striped Bass of the Atlantic Coast from Maine to North Carolina, wild striped bass are being closely monitored, with the goal of enhancing the wild striped bass stock throughout its Atlantic coast range.

✦ ✦ ✦

Although farmed-raised is the preferred choice when choosing striped bass, both farm-raised and wild striped bass are excellent eating fish and may be prepared in many ways. Smaller fish are usually fried and the larger ones baked.

Striped Bass with Orange, Thyme and Rum Mojo

Striped Bass with Orange, Thyme and Rum Mojo

Chef Allen Susser, Chef Allen's, Miami, Florida

◆

1 whole striped bass or 4 striped bass fillets (6 ounces each), skin on ▪ 2 teaspoons cumin seeds ▪ 1 teaspoon coriander seeds ▪ 1 teaspoon whole black peppercorns ▪ 1 tablespoon salt ▪ 1 teaspoon thyme ▪ 3 tablespoons olive oil ▪ ½ cup sweet onion, diced ▪ 1 tablespoon garlic, minced ▪ 1 cup fresh orange juice ▪ ¼ cup fresh lime juice ▪ ¼ cup spiced dark rum ▪ 1 medium orange, segmented ▪ 1 tablespoon chopped cilantro

To prepare the striped bass: In a dry pan, over medium heat, toast the cumin seeds, coriander seeds, and whole black peppercorns until aromatic, approx 1 to 2 minutes. Crush the spices. Use these along with salt and thyme to season the striped bass well on both sides. Drizzle with 1 tablespoon olive oil, and set aside until ready to cook. To prepare the mojo: In a medium sauce pot add 1 tablespoon olive oil, onion and garlic. Cook until translucent, approx 3 minutes. Add the remaining toasted spices and stir well. Add the orange juice, lime juice, and about half of the rum. Bring to a boil and then lower to a simmer, cooking for 10 minutes. To cook the striped bass: Heat a large non-stick pan with remaining olive oil. Sauté the striped bass on each side, browning it well. Add the remaining rum. Cook bass until flesh is tender. To serve: Remove the fish from the heat to fish plates or a platter. Garnish with cilantro, orange segments, and serve with the mojo sauce. *Serves*

Striped Bass Panamanian Style with Salsa Criollo

Chef Julio Ramirez, The Fishwife at Asilomar Beach, Pacific Grove, California

◆

4 fresh striped bass fillets (6 ounces each, rinsed and patted dry) ▪ 1 teaspoon salt ▪ ¼ teaspoon freshly-ground black pepper ▪ 2 teaspoons peanut oil ▪ Salsa Criollo: 1 cup fresh pineapple, minced ▪ 2 tablespoons sugar ▪ 1 tablespoon peanut oil ▪ 1 medium onion, diced ▪ 1 tablespoon garlic, minced ▪ ¼ fresh chombo or habañero chile, minced ▪ 1 roasted pasilla chile and 1 red bell pepper, both seeded, de-veined and diced ▪ 2 cups diced tomatoes ▪ ½ cup water ▪ 1 tablespoon kosher salt ▪ 1 cup cherry tomatoes, quartered ▪ 2 tablespoons chopped cilantro

For the salsa criollo: Place pineapple in saucepan over medium heat; add sugar. Cook until sugar has melted and the liquids mix, about 15 minutes; reserve. Heat oil in a saucepan over medium heat, add onions, garlic and chile. Increase heat to medium-high; stir occasionally, about 4 minutes. Add remaining peppers. Stir well. Add diced tomatoes, stir well, and reduce heat to medium. Stir occasionally for 5 minutes. Add water and salt. Remove from heat. Add cherry tomatoes, cilantro and pineapple. For the fish: Take one fish fillet and cut in half along the spine. You will have 2 fillets; the dorsal fillet will be thicker than the other. Take dorsal half and butterfly it (split in half through the middle). You will now have 3 fillets of almost equal thickness. Repeat process with the remaining fillets. Dust with salt and pepper. Place 2 sauté pans over medium heat; add a teaspoon of oil to each and heat until pans are almost smoking. Add fillets, distributing them equally, and cook for 2 minutes. Sprinkle fillets with salt and pepper, then turn and cook for 2 minutes. Sprinkle with salt and pepper and remove from heat. To serve: Plate fish, topping each fillet with 3 tablespoons of Salsa Criollo. Accompany with rice, tostadas, and a green salad. *Serves four.*

Albacore

Thunnus alalunga

When buying albacore, ask for troll-caught or pole-caught. When buying canned albacore, the troll-caught or pole-caught fish has a slightly higher fat content—about four grams in comparison with the one gram in longlined albacore.

Albacore is a medium-sized tuna, inhabiting the world's temperate, subtropical, and tropical oceans. Distinguished by its long, graceful pectoral fins, the albacore is one of the most migratory of tunas. Albacore tunas range from 24–36 inches in length and 20–40 pounds in weight. They mature after a few years of age and can live up to ten years. They are dark blue on top with a lighter underbelly. Although albacore steaks are available, most of the albacore sold in U.S. markets is the higher-priced, canned variety.

Albacore tuna is the only tuna that can be canned under the "white meat" label. The meat has a somewhat dry texture, and the taste comes close to the taste of chicken meat. Due to the white color and taste of its meat, albacore is also referred to as "the chicken of the sea."

Today, the largest fraction of the world's albacore catch comes from the Pacific, with Japan, New Zealand, South Korea, Taiwan, and the United States harvesting the greatest amounts.

The United States, with an albacore fishing fleet of about 500 vessels, brings in approximately five to ten percent of the world's albacore catch. The U.S. boats troll-catch in colder waters, which means their albacore have a higher Omega 3 oil content than albacore caught by longline fleets fishing in tropical waters. This difference in fishing methods and water temperature are noticeable on the label. Troll-caught albacore canned by Bumble Bee (a U.S. corporation), Star Kist (U.S.) and Chicken of the Sea (Thailand), have more than four grams of fat per serving, whereas longline-caught albacore has only one gram of fat.

Though the albacore population seems to be healthy and stable, there are some problems with how the tuna are caught. The U.S. albacore fleet fishes in an environmentally-friendly manner with surface hook and line troll gear, which results in near-zero bycatch. There is considerable concern, however, about the amount and type of bycatch from longlining. Currently, the U.S. is the only Pacific fishing nation with provisions protecting sea turtles and albatrosses from the effects of tuna longlining. For this reason consumers should consider this "Good Alternatives" when it comes to tuna caught using longlines.

❖　❖　❖

When buying albacore, ask for troll-caught or pole-caught. Pole and troll (jig boats) fleets target younger, surface albacore, while the longline fishery targets the older, deep-swimming albacore.

Grilled Albacore on a Ragoût of Wild Mushrooms, Fiddlehead Ferns and Artichokes with Fresh Dungeness Crab and Bay Shrimp

CHEF WILHELM BORGSTROM, MCCORMICK & SCHMICK'S SEAFOOD RESTAURANT, Chicago, Illinois

◆

4 albacore steaks (6 ounces each) ▪ 8 large artichoke bottoms, cooked and quartered ▪ 8 fingerling or gold potatoes, cooked and halved ▪ 4 garlic cloves, slivered as thinly as possible ▪ 4 Roma tomatoes, peeled, seeded and diced ▪ 2 large fresh basil leaves, chiffonade ▪ 1 pound mixed fresh wild mushrooms (morels, chanterelles, shiitakes, and oyster mushrooms) ▪ 4 ounces fiddlehead ferns (or leeks if ferns are unavailable) ▪ 2 tablespoons lemon juice ▪ ¼ cup dry white wine ▪ 2 tablespoons olive oil ▪ 4 ounces cooked fresh dungeness crab ▪ 4 ounces cooked fresh bay shrimp ▪ 1 tablespoon whole butter ▪ kosher sea salt and cracked black pepper to taste ▪ chopped chives to garnish

Heat a grill to medium-high heat and lightly oil so the fish won't stick. Rub the albacore steaks with salt and cracked pepper. Be sure to press the pepper firmly into the fish so they don't fall off. Cook medium rare, preparing the ragoût while the fish cooks. In a large sauté pan, heat the olive oil until smoking. Sauté the potatoes and artichokes for one minute, until they start to brown. Add the mushrooms and slivered garlic. Sauté for one minute longer and add the white wine. Reduce the heat to a simmer and add the basil, tomatoes, and fiddlehead ferns or leeks. Allow the wine to reduce by half, then add the lemon juice and swirl in butter. Keep warm until ready to serve. Just before serving, melt the remaining butter in a small saucepan and warm the shrimp and crabmeat. TO SERVE: Place the ragoût in the center of 4 shallow bowls. Place the cooked albacore on top and spoon the crab and shrimp over the top, allowing a little to fall over the vegetables. Sprinkle with chopped chives and serve immediately. *Serves four.*

Warm Niçoise Salad

CHEF TED WALTER, PASSIONFISH RESTAURANT, Pacific Grove, California

◆

2 pounds fresh albacore, cut into 4 equal portions ▪ 1 tablespoon black peppercorns ▪ 1 tablespoon whole coriander ▪ 1 teaspoon kosher salt ▪ 1 red bell pepper, diced ▪ 2 handfuls haricot vert, trimmed, poached and cooled ▪ 2 small red onions, diced ▪ ¼ cup niçoise olives, pitted ▪ 1 pound red potatoes, steamed, cooled and cubed ▪ ½ pound artichoke hearts, boiled and cooled ▪ 1 bunch fresh basil, puréed ▪ 2 tablespoons extra virgin olive oil ▪ ½ cup red wine ▪ ½ cup fish stock

Grind peppercorns and coriander. Add salt and mix well. Roll tuna in the mix. Sauté the bell pepper and onion in olive oil until tender, then deglaze with wine. Add beans, potatoes, olives, and artichoke hearts. Add the fish stock and simmer until the vegetables are warm; set aside. Sear tuna on both sides until rare or desired preparation. Mix basil purée with vegetables. TO SERVE: Plate the vegetables. Cut each portion of tuna in half and place on top of vegetables. Serve immediately. *Serves four.*

Grilled Albacore on a Ragoût of Wild Mushrooms, Fiddlehead Ferns and Artichokes with Fresh Dungeness Crab and Bay Shrimp

Yellowfin Tuna

Thunnus albacares

Currently, the United States is the only Pacific fishing nation with provisions protecting sea turtles and albatrosses from the effects of tuna longlining.

Yellowfin is second only to albacore in terms of tuna volume. They are found in warmer waters in many oceans and seas except the Mediterranean. They are both pelagic and seasonally migratory, but have been known to come fairly close to shore. Their diet includes fish, flying fish, squid, and crustaceans.

The world's leading yellowfin tuna producers are Japan and the United States. Hawaii produces a consistently high-quality yellowfin, which they refer to as Ahi, meaning fire.

Yellowfin tuna have been recorded up to 400 pounds, but the range in the commercial catch is from 20 to 120 pounds. They're harvested by various methods, but the most common is by longline and purse seine. Dolphins were once caught in large numbers in seine nets set for tuna. As a result of

Seafood WATCH

The U.S. is the only Pacific fishing nation with provisions protecting sea turtles and albatrosses from the effects of tuna longlining. For this reason consumers should consider this "Good Alternatives" when it comes to tuna caught using longlines. When buying yellowfin or bigeye tuna, ask for troll-caught or pole-caught tuna. These methods take little bycatch and are therefore "Best Choices."

For current fishery status, visit www.seafoodwatch.org

this, many of the large tuna vessels today have modified their nets and fishing methods to correct this problem. However, species such as sharks, mahi-mahi, and other finfishes are now being incidentally caught. Therefore, when choosing yellowfin, select tuna that is longline or hook-and-line caught, two fishing methods that don't use seine nets. As a general rule, seined yellowfin is brine-frozen and canned, while longlined tuna is marketed fresh or frozen.

In today's fish markets, plenty of tuna loins are typically on hand, from which steaks are cut. Whether imported or domestic, tuna flesh of equal quality sells for the same price. Because of the migratory nature of this open-water fish, yellowfin prices tend to be at their lowest during the summer months (July through September) when yellowfin are in abundance, and at their highest during late winter and early spring (February through April) when catches are smaller.

For top quality tuna, look for steaks that have a deep red color, a slight translucence, and firm flesh. Tuna can lose its bright red color quickly so keep it refrigerated, well-wrapped, and out of contact with air or ice.

✦ ✦ ✦

Yellowfin is excellent for a wide variety of cooking methods. The main point to remember is not to overcook. This is generally true of all fish, but tuna's especially low fat content means the flesh can easily become dry and tough when overcooked. To keep the flesh moist and tasty, tuna is often at its best grilled, broiled or pan-seared; the high heat seals the outside, conserving the moisture and flavor inside. Tuna cooked only to rare or medium is particularly tender and succulent.

Peppercorn-Crusted Yellowfin Tuna with Saffron and Fava Bean Risotto

Peppercorn-Crusted Yellowfin Tuna with Saffron and Fava Bean Risotto

CHEF MARK HOLLEY, PESCE, HOUSTON, Texas

✦

4 yellowfin tuna fillets (6 ounces each) ▪ olive oil (as needed) ▪ Dijon mustard (as needed) ▪ crushed black peppercorns (as needed) ▪ **SAFFRON AND FAVA BEAN RISOTTO:** 3 pints shrimp stock ▪ 1 teaspoon saffron threads ▪ 4 tablespoons olive oil ▪ 2 tablespoons unsalted butter ▪ ¼ cup yellow onions, diced ▪ 2 cups arborio rice ▪ ¼ cup oyster mushrooms ▪ 2 cups fava beans, blanched ▪ 2 tablespoons Parmesan cheese, grated ▪ kosher salt and black pepper to taste ▪ **HERB OIL:** 2 ounces fresh parsley ▪ 1 ounce fresh tarragon ▪ 1 ounce fresh thyme ▪ 4 ounces olive oil ▪ balsamic vinegar, reduced to a syrup (as needed) ▪ 2 cups micro greens

To PREPARE THE RISOTTO: Bring the shrimp stock to a simmer and add the saffron threads. Heat half of the olive oil and half of the butter in a heavy saucepan and sauté the onions until they are golden. Add the rice and stir to coat it with the oil and butter. Over medium heat, add 4 ounces of the shrimp stock to the rice. Stir and cook until the liquid is absorbed. Add another portion of the stock, stir and cook, until the liquid is absorbed. Continue adding stock, one portion at a time, stirring often, until the rice is creamy but still firm in the center. The process will take approximately 20 minutes. FOR THE HERB OIL: Blanch the herbs in hot water for 10 seconds. Cook and dry thoroughly. Measure the volume of the herbs and put them in a blender. Add an equal amount of olive oil. Purée and strain through a mesh strainer. FOR THE TUNA: Heat the olive oil in a sauté pan. Brush the tuna with the Dijon mustard and sprinkle evenly with the crushed peppercorns to form a crust. Sear the tuna on each side until medium rare, approx 1 minute on each side. Remove and allow to rest. In a separate pan, sauté the mushrooms in the remaining olive oil until tender. Season with salt and pepper. Fold the mushrooms, fava beans, Parmesan cheese, and remaining butter into the risotto and season with salt and pepper. To SERVE: Place a ladle of Saffron and Fava Bean Risotto in the center of each plate. Drizzle the herb oil and balsamic vinegar reduction around the risotto. Slice the tuna fillets in half and place on top of the risotto. Place micro greens on top of tuna. *Serves four.*

Trevally Jack

Caranx ignobilis

Although it is highly sought as a food fish, the trevally jack can be known to have ciguatera poisoning—caused by consumption of reef fish that feed on certain dinoflagellates (i.e. algae) associated with coral reef systems.

Jacks are well represented in all tropical and subtropical seas, including the Hawaiian waters. They are part of the family *Carangidae,* which contains 25 genera and approximately 145 species.

Large jacks, like the trevally jack, form an important component of shallow water reef and lagoon fish catches throughout the Pacific Islands.

The trevally jack can be recognized by its steep head profile and its large size. It is the largest species of jack, growing to over three feet in length. They have a deep, robust body, and their color is generally olive green with a darker dorsal surface and a white belly that darkens considerably after capture.

Trevally jacks are pelagic fish usually seen cruising along the surface in near-shore habitats, including rocky shores, reefs, and bays. Trevally jacks are predators that prefer to feed at night. Their diet consists mostly of fish with the balance made up of squid, shrimp, and other crustaceans. Despite their importance to fisheries, little is known about the basic biology and habitat requirements of the trevally jack.

Trevally jacks are caught year-round in the Hawaiian Islands, and are usually available in the market. The smaller fish are available fresh on ice or frozen. Most of the larger specimens are filleted, and then sold fresh or frozen.

❖ ❖ ❖

In Hawaii, commercial fishing for trevally is conducted from vessels that usually target bottomfish, such as snapper and grouper. These vessels utilize handlines that are set and hauled on electric-, hydraulic- or hand-powered reels. Experienced bottom fishermen have the ability to catch desired species with little bycatch. However, it is impossible to completely avoid non-target species. Sharks, oilfish, snake mackerel, pufferfish, and moray eels are common bycatch species, discarded because they are not marketable.

Seafood WATCH

Although gear used to catch jacks is fairly selective, bycatch of undesirable species occurs frequently, with unknown ecosystem consequences. Management has been only moderately effective in regulating catch of this and other bottomfish to ensure sustained stocks. Considering such factors, trevally jack from Hawaii should be placed in the "Good Alternatives" category.

For current fishery status, visit www.seafoodwatch.org

Pan Seared Trevally Jack with Spicy Collards and Stone Ground Grits

CHEF MATT KARAS, THE PILOT HOUSE

✦

6 fresh trevally fillets (7–8 ounces each) ▪ sea salt and pepper to taste ▪ olive oil as needed ▪ FOR THE COLLARDS: 1 pound julienne collards ▪ ½ pound julienne country ham ▪ ½ cup hot sauce of choice ▪ 1 cup julienne red onion ▪ 1 cup julienne yellow squash ▪ 1 cup julienne red bell pepper ▪ ¼ cup apple cider vinegar ▪ ½ tablespoon fresh minced garlic ▪ FOR THE GRITS: 1¼ cup grits ▪ 4 cups milk ▪ 2 tablespoons butter ▪ salt and pepper to taste

In a large sauté pan over medium-high heat, sauté country ham and garlic in a small amount of olive oil. Cook for 5 minutes and add hot sauce, vinegar, and collards. Cook for 15 minutes, then add remaining ingredients. Cook for another 10 minutes; reserve. FOR THE GRITS: Combine all ingredients in a pan over medium-high heat, stirring frequently. When grits begin to thicken, heat and cook for 20 minutes. FOR THE FISH: Sauté fish over medium-high heat 4 to 5 minutes on each side. TO SERVE: Place fish fillets on a serving dish, along with the spicy collards and stone ground grits. *Serves six.*

Wok Charred Trevally Jack with Garlic Sesame Crust and Lime Ginger Beurre Blanc

CHEF JEAN MARIE JOSSELIN, A PACIFIC CAFÉ, Kauai, Hawaii

✦

8 trevally jack fillets (3 ounces each) ▪ salt and pepper to taste ▪ FOR THE GARLIC SESAME CRUST: ½ cup white sesame seeds ▪ 2 tablespoons minced garlic ▪ salt and pepper to taste ▪ 1 teaspoon corn starch ▪ FOR THE LIME GINGER SAUCE: 1 cup dry white wine ▪ 4 slices fresh ginger ▪ ½ cup heavy cream ▪ 3 limes, juiced ▪ 1 pound cold unsalted butter, cut in small cubes ▪ black sesame seeds for presentation

Prepare the Garlic Sesame Crust by combining the ingredients; mix well; reserve until ready to use. FOR THE LIME GINGER SAUCE: In a non-reactive pan, combine the white wine and the fresh slivers of ginger and reduce by half, at medium heat. Add the heavy cream and reduce by half. Add the cold cubes of butter one at a time until each one is incorporated into the reduction; make sure that the sauce does not boil, but keep the temperature of the sauce just below boiling at all times while you incorporate the butter. Pass through a strainer and place the sauce into a bar blender. Add the minced ginger, lime juice, salt and pepper if needed, and process at medium speed until the ginger and lime juice are incorporated into the sauce; reserve. Season the fish with salt and pepper on both sides. Add 1 tablespoon of the cold sesame butter on one side of the fish. Place a heavy-bottom skillet or a wok at high heat, and when the skillet is very hot, add the fish with the sesame crust first, cook for 2 minutes on each side, and reserve the fish until ready to use. TO SERVE: Place the fish in the center of a plate, accompanied by stir fried vegetables if desired. Drizzle the lime ginger butter sauce around the fish and sprinkle with black sesame seeds. *Serves four to eight.*

Pan Seared Trevally Jack with Spicy Collards and Stone Ground Grits

Opah

Lampris guttatus

Rising demand for fresh fish, particularly in the restaurant trade, has increased the interest in previously under-utilized species, like the opah.

Opah, or moonfish, is one of the most colorful of the commercial fish species available in California and Hawaii. A silvery-grey upper body color shades to a rose-red dotted with white spots toward the belly. Its fins are crimson, and its large eyes are encircled with gold. The moonfish's unique round yet narrow profile may be the origin of its name.

The opah was viewed as a good luck fish by old-time longline fishermen, who would give it away as a gesture of goodwill rather than sell it. Only recently has this species become commercially important.

Opah are not found in schools, and thus are not caught in any quantity. They are a wandering pelagic species, often found in the company of tunas and billfish. Individual fish are regularly hooked by longline boats fishing over seamounts. Landings follow no set pattern in any particular area, but

the presence of opah at the depths of longline fishing gear may be related to vertical migrations from the deep in search of food. Virtually all opah landed by longliners is sold fresh through the Honolulu fish auction. Moonfish landed in Hawaii range from 60 to over 200 pounds.

The entire opah catch is marketed as whole, fresh fish. Most are filleted for restaurant use, both in Hawaii and for export to the U.S. mainland.

Rising demand for fresh fish, particularly in the restaurant trade, has increased the interest in previously under-utilized species like the opah. This species has now found a place on restaurant menus as a "catch of the day," particularly when more popular species are unavailable.

✦   ✦   ✦

An opah has four types of large-grain flesh, each a different color. Behind the head and along the backbone is an orange flesh. Toward the belly, the flesh pales to a pink color and is somewhat stringy. The fish's cheeks yield dark red flesh. Inside the fish's breastplate is another, smaller section of flesh. A bright ruby red or liver color, this flesh cooks to a brown color and is somewhat stringy and difficult to fillet.

Spicy Hawaiian Opah Fish Cake with Pineapple Aïoli and Sweet and Sour Sauce

Spicy Hawaiian Opah Fish Cake with Pineapple Aïoli and Sweet and Sour Sauce

CHEF KEITH MADEIRA, NEPTUNE'S GARDEN RESTAURANT, PACIFIC BEACH HOTEL, Waikiki, Hawaii

✦

FOR THE FISH: 10 ounces opah fillet, diced into ¼" cubes ▪ 1 tablespoon pickled ginger, chopped ▪ ¼ bundle thin chiffonade or Thai basil ▪ 1½ teaspoons fresh ogo (seaweed), chopped ▪ ¼ cup mayonnaise ▪ ½ cup panko (Japanese bread crumbs) ▪ ¾ teaspoon garlic, chopped ▪ 2 eggs, lightly beaten ▪ flour (as needed) ▪ chili garlic paste (to taste, approx 1½ teaspoons) ▪ sea salt to taste ▪ FOR THE SWEET AND SOUR SAUCE: ½ cup pineapple, diced ▪ ¾ cup ketchup ▪ ¼ cup green bell pepper, seeds removed and diced ▪ 1½ tablespoons sweet onion, diced ▪ ¼ cup cane sugar ▪ 3 tablespoons chili garlic paste ▪ 1½ teaspoons or to taste macadamia nut oil (preferred) ▪ FOR THE PINEAPPLE AÏOLI: ½ cup pineapple, diced ▪ 2 tablespoons rice wine vinegar ▪ 1 egg, plus 1 additional yolk ▪ 1 tablespoon Dijon mustard ▪ 1½ cups canola oil ▪ sea salt to taste ▪ FOR THE PINEAPPLE SHAVINGS: ½ cup pineapple, thinly sliced ▪ ½ teaspoon kaffir lime leaf, finely minced ▪ ¼ Meyer lemon, finely-minced zest ▪ cane sugar to taste

Combine all of the fish ingredients into a mixing bowl except for the panko bread crumbs. Mix well and form 6, 3-ounce cakes. Place onto a plate and reserve. Lightly dust each cake with flour on all sides. Dip into egg mixture and remove. Place in panko bread crumbs and coat well on all sides. Place cakes onto a clean plate, cover with plastic wrap, and chill until ready to serve. FOR THE SWEET AND SOUR SAUCE: In a saucepan over medium-low heat, add a small amount of macadamia nut oil and sweat vegetables until onions are translucent. Add vinegar, ketchup, sugar, and chili paste. Mix well and bring to a simmer and cook until lightly thickened (approx. 25 minutes). Remove from heat and set aside to cool. Add cooled mixture to a blender and purée until smooth. Strain through a food mill or fine strainer and reserve liquid. Sauce should be thick enough to coat a spoon. Keep warm until ready to use. FOR THE PINEAPPLE AÏOLI: Combine the ingredients except the oil into a blender. Blend until smooth. While machine is running, slowly add oil until thickened to desired consistency. If mixture is too thick, add water to thin. Add salt to taste. Remove from blender and chill. FOR THE PINEAPPLE SHAVINGS: Combine ingredients into a mixing bowl. Cover and chill. TO PREPARE FISH: Preheat canola oil to 350°F. Crisp fry fish cakes until lightly brown on all sides. Remove cakes from oil and place on paper towel. TO SERVE: Ladle approx 1.5 ounces sweet and sour sauce in center of six appetizer plates. Place one fish cake in the center of each sauce. Drizzle pineapple aïoli over cakes. Garnish with shaved pineapple and micro greens. Sprinkle with sesame seeds. *Serves six.*

Mahi Mahi

Coryphaena hippurus

Mahi mahi is often thought of as a Hawaiian fish, but it is found worldwide in tropical and subtropical waters. In the western Atlantic, mahi mahi range from Nova Scotia to Brazil. They are also found throughout the Caribbean Sea, the Gulf of Mexico, and the warm waters of the Pacific Ocean. Mahi mahi are sometimes called dolphinfish or dorado, but should not be confused with dolphins, which are mammals.

The mahi mahi is famous for the brilliant waves of color when they are first taken from the water. Alive in the sea, its sides are iridescent blue and variously mottled and washed with gold, while its tail is a vivid golden-yellow.

At times, schools of mahi mahi can be found congregating beneath any sort of object floating in the water—such as wood or mats of sargassum weed. Larger males tend to be more solitary. Mahi mahi are considered to be dimorphic, meaning that males and females differ in appearance; males develop a large, bony crest on their foreheads but females do not.

It is believed that mahi mahi populations are abundant and healthy due to the rapid life cycle and high reproductive rate of the species. Most mahi mahi only live a year or two, although the oldest fish can live up to around four years of age. Maximum size can be up to five or six feet and almost 90

pounds. This fast growth rate—in excess of three feet in the first year—makes them one of the ocean's fastest-growing fish. They feed mostly on flying fish, mackerels, and jacks. Mahi mahi can spawn during their first year of growth and may reproduce several times during a single spawning season. This unusually fast growth rate and high reproductive rate may make mahi mahi less susceptible to overfishing than other longer-lived, slower-maturing fish. Still, management regulations are needed to help conserve this valuable fishery.

There is little bycatch associated with mahi mahi though, at one time, they were themselves bycatch in the tuna and swordfish fisheries. In the United States, most mahi mahi are caught by anglers using rod and reel.

✦ ✦ ✦

Mahi mahi is thin-skinned with firm, light-pink flesh. It has a delicate, mild flavor that is almost sweet. Fresh mahi mahi has a shelf life of ten days if properly cared for. The fish caught by trolling or pole-and-line are the preferred choice. They are also generally one or two days old and much fresher than mahi mahi caught by longline boats on extended trips. Mahi mahi is ideal for a variety of preparations. However, care should be taken not to overcook mahi mahi. It should be cooked until it flakes and no longer.

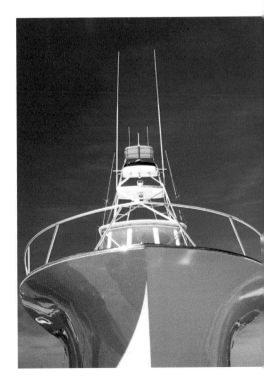

Seared Mahi Mahi with Orange and Fennel, Polenta and Fried Leeks

CHEF TIM FISHER, PORTOLA CAFÉ, Monterey, California

◆

4 fresh mahi mahi fillets (6 ounces each) ▪ 2 ounces olive oil ▪ 2 shallots, diced ▪ 2 cloves garlic, sliced ▪ 1 tablespoon fresh ginger, chopped ▪ 2 heads fennel, core removed, julienne ▪ 2 ounces white wine ▪ 3 oranges, sectioned with pith removed ▪ 4 ounces fresh-squeezed orange juice ▪ 3 tablespoons butter ▪ salt and pepper to taste ▪ FOR THE POLENTA: ½ cup polenta ▪ 3 cups water ▪ 3 tablespoons Parmesan cheese ▪ 2 tablespoons butter ▪ salt and pepper to taste ▪ FOR THE LEEKS: 1 large leek ▪ 1 cup oil ▪ flour as needed ▪ salt and pepper to taste

Season mahi mahi with salt and pepper. Sear in hot oil on both sides until lightly brown (approx. 3 minutes per side). Mahi mahi should be medium-rare; reserve. Drain excess oil from pan, add shallots and sauté until brown and tender. Add ginger, garlic, and fennel, toss lightly. Add wine and continue cooking until fennel is tender and wine is almost completely reduced. Add orange juice, salt and pepper to taste. When orange juice comes to a boil, whip in butter, add orange segments, and remove from heat. FOR THE POLENTA: Bring water to a boil in a heavy saucepan. Add ½ teaspoon salt, then add polenta slowly, stirring with a wire whip. Lower heat to a simmer and cook polenta until thick and shiny. Add butter, cheese, and salt and pepper to taste. FOR THE LEEKS: Slice leek in half lengthwise, cut into 2-inch pieces and julienne-slice. Season flour with salt and pepper; dust leek strips. Heat oil to 350°F and fry leeks until brown and crispy. TO SERVE: Place polenta in center of plate, arrange mahi mahi around polenta, spoon over sauce, top with fried leeks, and serve. *Serves four.*

Pan-Seared Mahi Mahi with Shiitake, Tomato and Fresh Salad with Jasmine Rice Cake

CHEF JAMISON BRANDT, LAKE CRESCENT LODGE - "A FOREVER RESORT," Port Angeles, Washington

◆

4 fresh fillets of mahi mahi (3-ounces each, skin off) ▪ FOR THE SHIITAKE, TOMATO, AND FRESH SALAD: 4 cups shiitake mushrooms, stemmed and julienne ▪ 1 cup Roma tomatoes, diced ▪ ½ cup red onion, diced ▪ ½ teaspoon chopped garlic ▪ 1 cup fresh basil, chiffonade ▪ ½ cup rice vinegar ▪ 1 tablespoon sesame seed oil ▪ ½ teaspoon chili oil. ▪ FOR THE WASABI CREAM: 1 tablespoon wasabi paste ▪ ½ cup sour cream. ▪ FOR THE JASMINE RICE CAKE: 1 cup jasmine rice ▪ 3 cups water ▪ 2 ounces enoki mushrooms ▪ 2 ounces daikon radish sprouts

FOR THE SHIITAKE SALAD: Sauté julienne shiitake mushrooms in olive oil, and salt and pepper to taste; set aside and let cool. Combine the tomatoes, red onions, basil, garlic, rice vinegar, sesame seed oil, and chili oil in a mixing bowl. After mushrooms have cooled, add them to this mixture and set aside at room temperature. FOR THE WASABI CREAM: Whisk together wasabi paste and sour cream; set aside at room temperature. FOR THE JASMINE RICE CAKE: Bring rice to a boil, turn to simmer and cover (until sticky enough to mold). Put 5 ounces of rice in a 4-inch round mold and compact with the back of a spoon. Pull out of mold and put on griddle or in a sauté pan to brown on medium heat. Salt and pepper mahi mahi and pan sear medium-rare to medium. TO SERVE: Place rice cake onto center of the plates, arrange the two mahi fillets on top. Place shiitake salad in three corners of the plate. Garnish with enoki mushrooms, daikon radish sprouts, and wasabi cream. *Serves two.*

Seared Mahi Mahi with Orange and Fennel, Polenta and Fried Leeks

Wahoo

Acanthocybium solandri

Although bycatch in the Atlantic and Gulf of Mexico fisheries is low, bycatch does include threatened, endangered, or protected species such as sea turtles.

Wahoo (referred to as ono in Hawaii, meaning "good to eat") is a close relative of the king mackerel. They are slender, pelagic fish with finely serrated, triangular teeth and beak-like snouts.

They are distributed worldwide in tropical and subtropical waters. Those caught in the Hawaii troll fishery are the best seafood choice as there is little bycatch, the species is abundant, and the local fishery is well managed.

The body of a wahoo is dark blue or green on the dorsal, with 24 or more wavy cobalt blue bars running vertically along the sides. The belly and lower sides are silver. Wahoo may grow to more than 100 pounds, but the usual size of a Hawaiian wahoo is eight to 30 pounds.

Seafood WATCH

Wahoo grow and mature quickly, so they likely can withstand concentrated fishing pressure. However, there is concern because this fish has never had a scientific stock assessment and it is unknown if overfishing is presently occurring. Several regulatory measures have been introduced to reduce bycatch, but it is too early to tell if these regulations are helping to rebuild sea turtle stocks. For these reasons wahoo is on the "Good Alternatives" list.

For current fishery status, visit www.seafoodwatch.org

The wahoo is pelagic, living alone or forming small, loose aggregations. They congregate near drifting objects and move with the changing seasons, traveling into cooler waters during warm summer months. Wahoo feed on a variety of fishes, as well as squid. They have been recorded swimming in short bursts of up to 50 miles per hour, allowing for quick capture of prey species.

About half of the commercial wahoo landed in Hawaii are caught by trollers. The remainder are caught on longline gear. Troll-caught and longline wahoo are marketed through fish auctions in Honolulu and Hilo, where much of the catch is shipped directly to restaurants in Hawaii and the U.S. mainland.

✦ ✦ ✦

Since it is not possible for restaurants to offer fresh, local-caught fish such as mahi mahi throughout the year, chefs have turned to wahoo as a savory alternative. Wahoo flesh is whiter, flakier, and has a delicate texture and milder taste than the meat of other fast-swimming, pelagic species. Although wahoo may make oceanic migrations as far as those of tuna and marlin, it contains less of the strong-tasting "blood meat" muscle that the latter species use for long-distance swimming.

Although wahoo is versatile in its uses, cooking methods suitable for "lean" fish (those with low fat content) are recommended so that the flesh does not dry out when cooked. One way to retain moisture in a lean fish is by poaching.

Grilled Wahoo with Key Lime Cilantro Cream Sauce

Grilled Wahoo with Key Lime Cilantro Cream Sauce

KEY WEST SEAFOOD, Key West, Florida

✦

4 fresh wahoo fillets (6 ounces each) ▪ FOR THE SAUCE: ½ cup chopped cilantro stems ▪ ½ cup white wine ▪ 3 tablespoons vinegar ▪ 3 tablespoons Key lime juice ▪ 1 bay leaf ▪ 5 black peppercorns ▪ 1 teaspoon sugar ▪ 1 cup heavy cream ▪ ½ cup unsalted butter

FOR THE SAUCE: Mix all the ingredients in a saucepan, except for the butter and cream, and reduce to half. Add cream and reduce by half. Remove from heat and beat in butter, 1 tablespoon at a time. Strain and reserve. FOR THE FISH: Heat a grill or broiler.

Lightly brush wahoo fillets with olive oil and salt and pepper. Grill or broil for 8 to 10 minutes, or until fish is white and flaky when pierced with a fork. TO SERVE: Place fish on serving dish and spoon Key Lime Cilantro Cream Sauce over the top. *Serves four.*

Grilled Wahoo with Basil Vinaigrette and Hawaiian Avocado Relish

CHEF JEAN-MARIE JOSSELIN, A PACIFIC CAFÉ, Kauai, Hawaii

✦

4 fresh fillets of wahoo (8 ounces each) ▪ ½ cup macadamia nut oil ▪ 1 lime, juiced ▪ salt and pepper to taste ▪ FOR THE BASIL VINAIGRETTE: ¼ cup red wine ▪ ¾ cup macadamia nut oil ▪ ¼ cup fresh basil leaves, chopped ▪ 1 lime, juiced ▪ 3 teaspoons fresh ginger, chopped ▪ salt and pepper to taste ▪ FOR THE AVOCADO RELISH: 2 large tomatoes, peeled, seeded, and cut into small cubes ▪ 1 medium avocado, peeled and cut into small cubes ▪ 2 teaspoons fresh ginger, julienne cut ▪ 1 cup Hawaiian ogo (seaweed), chopped ▪ 24 asparagus, cooked, cut into 2 inch lengths ▪ salt and pepper to taste

Prepare basil vinaigrette by combining red wine vinegar, salt and pepper in a bowl. Mix well. Add lime juice, basil and ginger. Slowly add macadamia nut oil and mix well. Set aside. FOR THE RELISH: Combine tomato and avocado in a medium bowl; add seaweed, asparagus, ginger, salt and pepper. Add vinaigrette and toss lightly to blend. Set aside at room temperature. FOR THE WAHOO: Combine macadamia nut oil, lime juice, salt and pepper. Mix well and brush on both sides of fillets. Grill fish for 3 minutes on each side, or until medium-rare. TO SERVE: Place fish in center of plate and garnish with the avocado relish. *Serves four.*

Wreckfish

Polyprion americanus

WRECKFISH

Wreckfish are caught by hydraulic hook and line, a method that results in little bycatch and does not have adverse impacts on the ecosystem. In the United States, a management plan has been effective in maintaining healthy wreckfish stocks.

I n recent years, a new fishery has developed for a species that was formerly unknown or considered rare in the western North Atlantic—the wreckfish.

The wreckfish is a large, bottom-dwelling fish similar to a grouper. It is found in many temperate oceans around the world. Juvenile wreckfish live amidst floating seaweeds and wreckage, giving it the common name "wreck" fish. Wreckfish commonly exceed three feet in length and over sixty pounds in weight. Adult wreckfish live in depths from 100 to over 3,000 feet.

The U.S. fishery for wreckfish is in the Atlantic Ocean off South Carolina. The majority of the population inhabits deep, rocky outcrops and ledges near the Charleston Bump area, which is part of the Blake Plateau. Here, an underwater landscape deflects the warm Gulf Stream waters offshore, causing upwelling of bottom waters. Such upwelling increases the food supply and so supports large numbers of these big fish at depths that are usually food-poor.

The southeastern U.S. fishery began in 1987. Many of the boats are similar to those used in the southeastern snapper-grouper fishery. The wreckfish is fished in areas of moderate to strong current using two to four heavy-duty hydraulic reels spooled with thick cable. The fishing end of the cable is a rig consisting of 50 to 100 pounds of weight and eight to 20 large circle hooks baited with squid. The gear is fished just above the bottom. Although wreckfish are thought to mature slowly and live 30 years or more, their ability to produce a lot of offspring increases their resistance to fishing pressure. In the United States, a management plan has been effective in maintaining healthy wreckfish stocks.

✦ ✦ ✦

The wreckfish has no other distinct name except "sea bass." Wreckfish are sold fresh or frozen as a market substitute for snapper or grouper. The fishery is open from April to January of each year. Depending on the fishing effort, fresh wreckfish is available during those times.

Seafood WATCH

Although wreckfish are thought to mature slowly and live 30 years or more, their ability to produce a lot of offspring increases their resistance to fishing pressure. Wreckfish are caught by hydraulic hook and line, a method that results in little bycatch and does not have adverse impacts on the ecosystem. In the U.S., a management plan has been effective in maintaining healthy wreckfish stocks. For these reasons, wreckfish is a "Best Choice."

For current fishery status, visit www.seafoodwatch.org

Pecan-Crumb Crusted Wreckfish

CHEF ROBERT CARTER, THE PENINSULA GRILL, Charleston, South Carolina

✦

4 fresh wreckfish fillets (7 ounces each) ▪ 1 cup pecan nuts ▪ 1 cup plain bread crumbs ▪ 1 egg, lightly beaten ▪ 3 ounces olive oil ▪ FOR THE TOMATO BROTH: 6 tomatoes, rough chop ▪ 1 medium onion, rough chop ▪ 1 large carrot, rough chop ▪ 1 leek, rough chop ▪ 2 stalks celery, rough chop ▪ 1 bay leaf ▪ 4 garlic cloves ▪ ½ cup tomato juice ▪ 6 basil stems ▪ 2 tablespoons Chinese chili paste ▪ 1 quart water ▪ salt and white pepper to taste ▪ FOR THE CRAWFISH-ORZO PILAF: 2 ounces tomato broth ▪ 2 tablespoons shallots, minced ▪ 2 teaspoons garlic, minced ▪ ¼ cup bell peppers, small dice ▪ 12 ounces orzo pasta, cooked ▪ 8 ounces crawfish, cooked tail meat ▪ 1 tablespoon basil, chopped ▪ 1 tablespoon chives, chopped ▪ salt and white pepper to taste

Begin with preparing the tomato broth. Combine all ingredients in a medium saucepan. Bring to a boil. Reduce heat and simmer for 30 minutes. Strain and season. FOR THE CRAWFISH-ORZO: Heat 2 ounces of the tomato broth in a medium saucepan with shallots and garlic. Add the peppers and cooked orzo (prepare according to package directions); heat through. Add crawfish, basil and chives. Season with salt and white pepper. FOR THE FISH: In a food processor, grind pecan nuts and bread crumbs together until fine crumb. Dip top of wreckfish into egg wash and then into nut crumb mixture. In a medium sauté pan over medium heat, sauté fish in olive oil until nuts are lightly golden. Turn fish and finish in 400°F oven for 3 minutes or until done. TO SERVE: Place wreckfish fillet on a bed of Crawfish-Orzo. *Serves four.*

NOTE: A large portion of tomato broth will be left over. Use the delicious broth for a vegetable soup stock or freeze for later use.

Grilled Wreckfish with Jalapeño, Gouda Cheese Grits, and Black Bean Mango Salsa

CHEF PEYTON SMITH FISH RESTAURANT, *in association with the* **South Carolina Aquarium, Charlestown, South Carolina**

✦

8-ounce fresh wreckfish fillet ▪ 2 roasted jalapeños, peeled, seeded and diced ▪ ½ smoked gouda cheese, shredded ▪ 1 cup stone ground grits ▪ 1 cup water ▪ ½ cup heavy cream ▪ 1 tablespoon whole butter ▪ salt and pepper to taste ▪ FOR THE MANGO SALSA: 2 mangos, diced ▪ 2 cups black beans, cooked ▪ 1 red bell pepper, diced ▪ 1 green bell pepper, diced ▪ 1 bunch fresh cilantro, minced ▪ 1 tablespoon vegetable oil ▪ 2 tablespoons cider vinegar ▪ salt and pepper to taste

Prepare mango salsa by combining all ingredients in a bowl; mix well and reserve. FOR THE JALAPENO AND GOUDA CHEESE GRITS: In a medium saucepan, bring water and cream to a boil; season with salt and pepper. Add butter and allow to melt; add jalapeños. While stirring continuously, add grits and reduce heat to simmer. When grits are tender, add cheese; season with salt and pepper to taste; reserve. FOR THE WRECKFISH: Season and sauté fillet until golden brown on both sides and remove from heat. TO SERVE: Generously spoon grits onto 2 serving dishes and divide fish fillet on top of grits. Garnish with Black Bean and Mango Salsa. *Serves two.*

Pecan-Crumb Crusted Wreckfish

CRUSTACEANS

Dungeness Crab

Cancer magister

Harvest methods in the dungeness crab fishery are very "targeted," resulting in little bycatch mortality. Only mature male crabs measuring a certain length are harvested. Undersized male crabs are returned to the ocean to insure a healthy "breed stock." All female crabs are released unharmed, where they can continue the mating cycle to insure healthy stocks and future harvests.

Dungeness crabs, named after a small fishing village on the Strait of Juan de Fuca in Washington State, have been harvested commercially along the Pacific Coast since the late 1800s. They range from central California to the Gulf of Alaska, and have long been part of the Northwest's seafood heritage.

Dungeness crabs inhabit eel-grass beds and muddy to sandy bottoms, from the low intertidal zone to depths in excess of 600 feet. They can be found from the Aleutian Islands in Alaska to south of San Francisco. While crabs measuring ten inches across the back have been taken off the coast

of Washington, they seldom exceed eight inches and average just under seven inches of shell width. They have white-tipped claws and a brownish-red shell.

Dungeness crabs eat a wide variety of marine life. Stomachs of these crabs have been found to contain clams, fish, and crabs, as well as other items, including starfish, worms, squid, snails, and eggs from fish or crabs. They are also cannibalistic.

Dungeness crabs are caught in circular steel traps commonly called "pots" weighing anywhere from 60 to 125 pounds. The pots are baited with herring, squid, and razor clams to attract the bottom-dwelling crabs during the one-to-three day "soak" period. Dungeness crabs are kept alive in tanks until they are delivered to a shore-side processor. Only male crabs measuring at least six and one-half inches across the shell may be harvested. Small males and all females are returned alive to the sea. The average boat fishes 250 to 300 pots, in depths ranging from five to 30 fathoms (30 to 180 feet) of water. These simple management measures have kept West Coast dungeness crab stocks healthy for the last 30 years.

✦ ✦ ✦

Served hot or chilled, dungeness crab has a sweet flavor and flaky texture that lends itself to a wide variety of preparation methods, from the simple to the elegant. Its moist white meat is as versatile as it is delicious.

Dungeness Crab Cakes with Field Greens and Garlic Aïoli

CHEF AND AUTHOR JAMES O. FRAIOLI, Santa Barbara, California

♦

3 cups fresh dungeness crab meat (picked and cleaned) ▪ 1½ cups Italian bread crumbs ▪ 1½ tablespoons fresh Italian parsley, chopped ▪ 2 tablespoons shallot, chopped ▪ garlic chili sauce (as needed, approximately 2 tablespoons) ▪ 1 to 2 tablespoons mayonnaise (optional) ▪ salt and pepper to taste ▪ olive oil for cooking ▪ fresh chives for garnish ▪ FOR THE GARLIC AÏOLI: 6 cloves garlic ▪ 3 tablespoons olive oil ▪ ⅓ cup sour cream ▪ ⅓ cup mayonnaise ▪ ¾ teaspoon lemon juice ▪ 1½ stalks chives, chopped ▪ sea salt and course black pepper to taste

In a large bowl, combine fresh crab meat, Italian bread crumbs, parsley and chopped shallot. Fold in garlic chili sauce until desired taste is achieved. Add a dash or two of sea salt and course black pepper. With wet hands, form 4 to 6 crab cakes depending on serving amount. Heat olive oil in a large sauté pan over medium heat. Meanwhile, prepare garlic aïoli by combining ingredients in a small mixing bowl and stir until blended; set aside. To cook crab cakes, place cakes in heated pan (do not crowd in pan) until golden brown on each side. TO SERVE: Place one crab cake on a bed of fresh field greens. Top with Garlic Aïoli Sauce. Garnish with fresh chives. *Serves four to six.*

Dungeness Crab Club Sandwich on Toasted Brioche

CHEF CAPRIAL PENCE, WESTMORELAND BISTRO, Portland, Oregon, *in association with the* Oregon Dungeness Crab Commission

♦

2 cups fresh dungeness crab meat, picked ▪ fresh brioche bread (to make 12 slices) ▪ fresh tomatoes (as needed) ▪ red leaf lettuce (as needed) ▪ fresh chives (as needed) ▪ 1 red bell pepper, cut into strips ▪ FOR THE BASIL-THYME MAYONNAISE: ¼ cup white wine vinegar ▪ 2 shallots, finely chopped ▪ 2 garlic cloves, finely chopped ▪ 2 tablespoons Dijon-style mustard ▪ ¾ cup prepared mayonnaise ▪ 1 tablespoon fresh basil, finely chopped ▪ 1 tablespoon fresh thyme, finely chopped ▪ salt and pepper to taste

FOR THE MAYONNAISE: In a mixer or food processor fitted with a metal blade, place vinegar, shallots, garlic, mustard and mayonnaise. Pulse to blend. Add herbs and seasoning and pulse to mix. Refrigerate until needed. TO SERVE: Assemble the open-faced sandwiches by mixing crab meat with ½ cup Basil-Thyme Mayonnaise. Spread remaining ¼ cup of mayonnaise on toasted bread slices (12 slices). Layer toast with lettuce leaves, tomato slices and crab mixture. Garnish the top of the sandwich with chive strips and julienne red pepper. *Serves six.*

Dungeness Crab Cakes with Field Greens and Garlic Aïoli

Alaska Red King Crab

Paralithodes camtschaticus

The king crab is the largest crab in U.S. waters. They are characterized by their massive size and long spidery legs and spiny exteriors. There are three common species of king crab—red king crab, blue king crab, and brown (golden) king crab. Red king crab is the most sought after. The meat is the sweetest, and the legs are always packed full.

Red king crab also has the greatest distribution of the three species. In Asian waters, this species occurs from the Sea of Japan northward into the Sea of Okhotsk and along the shores of the Kamchatka Peninsula. In the northeast Pacific, distribution extends northward from British Columbia to Alaska and the Bering Sea. Red king crabs were intentionally transplanted into the North Atlantic during the 1960s. These crabs have naturalized, are breeding, and are now widely distributed along the Atlantic coasts of Russia and Norway.

Seafood WATCH

While about 50 percent of U.S. king crab stocks are considered "not overfished," crabs are recovering from previous decades of being caught faster than they could reproduce. Though Alaska's king crab fisheries are well managed, the abundance of king crab is unknown, giving the species a "Good Alternatives" rating. King crabs imported from Russia, where management laws are poorly enforced, should be "Avoided."

For current fishery status, visit www.seafoodwatch.org

King crabs feed on a wide assortment of marine life, including worms, clams, mussels, snails, brittle stars, sea stars, sea urchins, sand dollars, barnacles, fish parts, sponges and algae, as well as crabs (including king crabs) and other crustaceans. The red king crabs forage from the intertidal zone to depths of 100 fathoms or more.

King crabs are typically caught in large steel pots which are baited with chopped herring. Each pot weighs over 700 pounds when empty. The pots are set and retrieved using hydraulic launchers and large winches. Crab fishing in the Bering Sea still ranks as the nation's most dangerous job. Brave fishermen constantly battle harsh weather conditions and hazardous environments in their pursuit of the king crab.

❖ ❖ ❖

Most of the king crab on the U.S. market is currently supplied by Russian Far East fisheries, where management is very poor and stocks are severely overfished. Therefore, imported king crab should be avoided. King crab from Alaska is the better choice, although Alaska king crab stocks have also been overfished. Today, the Alaskan king crab fishery is well managed and fishing grounds are closed in many areas to allow stocks to recover.

King crab is delivered live to the docks, but almost all of the catch is cleaned and cooked before being marketed. King crab is commonly available frozen, as cooked "sections" (legs and thorax) or separate legs and claws. King crab is also marketed fresh-cooked in sections, legs, claws, and picked meat. Frozen king crab is available year-round.

Marinated Alaska King Crab

Marinated Alaska King Crab

FISHERMAN'S EXPRESS, Anchorage, Alaska

◆

Cooked Alaska king crab legs and claws (2 or 3 legs per person) ▪ FOR THE MARINADE: 1 cup olive oil ▪ 6 tablespoons white wine vinegar ▪ 2 limes, juiced ▪ 2 cloves garlic, minced ▪ ½ tablespoon Tabasco sauce ▪ 2 teaspoons each of freshly chopped oregano, basil, and Italian parsley ▪ ¼ teaspoon dried dill ▪ sea salt and course black pepper to taste

TO PREPARE THE MARINADE: Combine all the ingredients and stir until blended. To marinate the crab, place the legs and claws in the bottom of a large, shallow dish. Cover with the marinade, cover, and refrigerate overnight. TO SERVE: Drain and reserve the marinade. Arrange the legs and claws on a serving platter. Serve the marinade as a dipping sauce.

King Crab Bisque

FISHERMAN'S EXPRESS, ALASKA SEAFOODS, Anchorage, Alaska

◆

1 pound king crab meat ▪ 2 tablespoons white onion, finely chopped ▪ ¼ cup melted butter or margarine ▪ 3 tablespoons all purpose flour ▪ ¼ teaspoon paprika ▪ 1 quart milk ▪ ground white pepper and salt to taste ▪ fresh parsley, chopped, as needed

Remove any pieces of shell or cartilage from the crab meat. Break meat into small pieces. Sauté onion in butter until tender and golden. Blend in flour and seasonings. Add milk gradually, stirring constantly. Stir and cook until thick. Add crab meat and heat thoroughly. TO SERVE: Ladle crab bisque in large soup bowls and garnish with a pinch of fresh parsley. *Serves two to four.*

Snow Crab

Chionoecetes opilio

SNOW CRAB

Snow crab populations vary widely year to year, as the survival of young crabs depends on favorable water and weather conditions. Snow crabs are caught in traps, a method considered eco-friendly because fishermen can release undersized crabs and other bycatch relatively unharmed.

The snow crab, also called opilio or tanner crab, is a crustacean with a flat and almost circular body, slightly wider in the back. They are smaller than king crabs and, instead of the king's three sets of walking legs, have four sets of walking legs, plus a pair of claws.

The fully-grown male snow crab can be more than twice as large as the female, with a leg span usually less than two feet and a total weight of one to two pounds. Harvesting of females is prohibited by law and only the males of the commercially acceptable and legal minimum size are harvested.

Snow crabs are usually taken over sandy seafloor at depths ranging from 30 to 1,500 feet. Snow crabs are captured using large metal-framed traps, also called pots. The pots are baited with chopped herring and are left to soak and catch crabs for one to three days before being hauled aboard. Vessels for snow crabs range from small inshore boats to enormous "super crabbers," which ply the Bering Sea.

Atlantic populations of snow crab appear to be recovering from a decline in 1999. However, Pacific stocks do not seem to be recovering. The Bering Sea snow crab stock, which supplies the bulk of Alaskan snow crab, is heavily if not overfished. The United States is attempting to stabilize the Alaskan fishery with new quota systems. Canada, meanwhile, has had individual quota systems in

Seafood WATCH

In the U.S., Alaska has the largest snow crab fishery. Snow crab populations fished off Alaska's coast began to decline in 1999 and have not yet recovered. Although the fishery is well managed and is working to reverse the decline, Alaska snow crab remains in the "Good Alternatives" category. Canada, however, is the major source for U.S. imports, and maintains a healthy population, receiving a "Best Choice" rating.

For current fishery status, visit www.seafoodwatch.org

place for some years and appears to have stabilized its fishery. Together, the United States and Canada account for the majority of the snow crab on the U.S. market. Denmark (Greenland) and Russia supply the rest. Such "imported" snow crab should be avoided as fraud and illegal fishing are considered rampant in its Far East fisheries. Although Denmark is known for its advanced and progressive management regimes, the status of Greenland snow crab stocks are unknown.

❖ ❖ ❖

Noted for its sweet, delicate flavor, snowy-white meat, and tender texture, snow crab is a versatile seafood choice for a variety of convenient appetizers, salads, entrées, soups and sandwiches. Low in fat and calories, snow crab is high in protein and is an excellent source of vitamin A.

Beer-Steamed Snow Crab with Shallot Cream Sauce

ALASKA SEAFOOD MARKETING INSTITUTION, Juneau, Alaska

◆

4 Alaska snow crab clusters, thawed if necessary ▪ 3½ quarts cold water ▪ 12 ounces beer of choice ▪ French fries or oven fries (as needed) ▪ cider vinegar (as needed) ▪ FOR THE SHALLOT CREAM SAUCE (1 CUP): 3 tablespoons minced shallots ▪ 1 tablespoon butter ▪ 1 tablespoon flour ▪ ⅛ teaspoon each of crushed dill weed and black pepper ▪ ½ cup sour cream ▪ sea salt to taste

In a large pot, bring water and beer to a boil. Add Alaska snow crab and cook for 5 minutes, or until well heated. FOR THE SHALLOT CREAM SAUCE: Sauté the minced shallots in the butter until softened. Stir in the flour, crushed dill weed and pepper. Cook and stir about one minute. Blend in sour cream and add sea salt to taste. TO SERVE: Place crab clusters on serving platter and serve with French fries and cider vinegar. *Serves two to four.*

Snow Crab Wrap Sandwich

ALASKA SEAFOOD MARKETING INSTITUTE, Juneau, Alaska

◆

1 pound Alaska snow crab meat, out of shell, thawed ▪ 4 whole wheat flour tortillas (12 to14-inch), warmed ▪ 4 ounces Brie cheese, ripe, diced ▪ 4 cups mixed baby lettuce ▪ 1 cup tomato, diced ▪ 4 slices bacon, cooked ▪ ½ cup low fat mayonnaise ▪ 1½ teaspoon fresh dill, chopped

Mix the dill and mayonnaise together in a bowl. Place crab meat and Brie in a sauté pan; warm over medium heat until crab is warm and cheese starts to melt. Lay out the warm tortillas and spread 1 ounce of the dill mayonnaise mixture over each. Top with ¼ of the crab and Brie mixture, 1 cup of the mixed lettuce, ¼ cup diced tomato and 1 slice of bacon, lightly chopped. TO SERVE: Fold in the ends of the wrap and roll up like a cigar. Cut in half and plate. *Serves four.*

Beer-Steamed Alaska Snow Crab with Shallot Cream Sauce

Blue Crab

Callinectes sapidus

BLUE CRAB

There are three centers of blue crab fishing in the United States: Chesapeake Bay; the Southeast Atlantic coast; and the Gulf of Mexico. Each region supplies about a third of total domestic landings. Presently, blue crab populations are in decline in the Chesapeake Bay, stock status is unknown along the Southeast coast, and stocks may be declining in the Gulf of Mexico.

The olive-green and white "blue crab"—so named for its vivid blue claws—is a bottom-dwelling predator. It occupies a variety of habitats in fresh and brackish waters, as well as shallow oceanic waters along the coasts of the Western Atlantic, the Caribbean and the Gulf of Mexico.

Like its cousins the shrimp and crayfish, the blue crab has ten legs. It walks sideways using the three middle pairs and uses its front pincer claws for defending itself and securing food. The crab earns its scientific name from the remaining pair. *Callinectes*, in Greek, means "beautiful swimmer" and the blue crab's hind legs, shaped like paddles, make it a remarkable swimmer.

Adult blue crabs are omnivorous, they feed on bivalves, crustaceans, fish, marine worms, plants, detritus, and nearly any food item they can find (including dead fish and plants).

The primary producing states for blue crab are Maryland, North and South Carolina, and Louisiana. Maryland produces a more expensive, higher-quality blue crab because its cold waters and estuaries produce crabs high in flavorful fat. Carolina blue crabs are considered second to Maryland, while Louisiana provides options for price-sensitive customers who like a larger crab.

Blue crabs are commercially caught with baited traps. The blue crab fishery is well managed but relies on the support of recreational fishermen. Note that a single female blue crab can produce up to eight million eggs in one mating season, so their capture should be minimal. Also, crab pots should not be left unattended for long periods of time, and only those crabs that will be eaten should be kept.

✦ ✦ ✦

Hard blue crabs are always marketed live. Crabs that have perished in transit should be immediately discarded since there is no reliable way to determine the degree of spoilage. Motion and heat are the biggest factors affecting mortality in transit. Male hard crabs are usually called "Jimmies," and mature female crabs are usually called "Sooks." Jimmies are generally larger and meatier, and are therefore more desirable for eating whole—either steamed or boiled. Sooks are often sold to commercial processing plants to be picked and packaged as fresh or pasteurized meat. Soft-shell crabs are one of America's favorite seafood delicacies. While all crabs shed their shells to grow, only a few species of crab can actually be eaten in this form. The blue crab is the only commercially available soft-shell product.

Soft Shell Crabs with Saké and Black Bean Sauce

Soft Shell Crabs with Saké and Black Bean Sauce

THE CRAB PLACE, Crisfield, Maryland

✦

8 fresh soft-shell crabs ▪ 4 tablespoons butter ▪ flour (as needed) ▪ 1 cup saké ▪ 4 green onions, minced ▪ 2 cloves garlic, minced or crushed ▪ 2 tablespoons fermented black beans, rinsed and chopped

Pat the crabs dry and dredge lightly in flour. Shake off excess. In a large skillet, melt 2 tablespoons butter over medium-high heat. Place 4 crabs in skillet, back-side down, and cook until lightly browned, about 2 minutes. Turn and cook until brown on other side. Remove to a heated platter and keep warm in a low oven. Cook remaining crabs in remaining 2 tablespoons butter in same fashion. Increase heat to high. Pour the saké into the skillet and bring to a boil, using a wooden spoon to scrape any browned bits out of the pan. Add the green onions and garlic and boil 1 minute until onions are limp. Add the black beans and boil 1 minute longer, stirring constantly. To SERVE: Place crabs on serving dish and spoon over sauce. *Serves four.*

French-Fried Jimmy Crabs

THE CRAB PLACE, Crisfield, Maryland

✦

12 medium-sized cooked male blue crabs (scrubbed and cleaned) ▪ 1 pound backfin crab meat ▪ 1 scant cup flour ▪ 1 scant cup milk ▪ 1 teaspoon salt ▪ 1 teaspoon celery seed ▪ 2 teaspoons parsley ▪ 1 egg ▪ 1 teaspoon Old Bay seasoning ▪ 1 tablespoon vegetable oil (enough for deep frying) ▪ lemons for garnish

Combine all ingredients except crab, crab meat, and vegetable oil to make a batter. Stir one tablespoon of vegetable oil into the batter. Fill crab crevices where innards were removed with crab meat and press the crab meat firmly into the crevice to secure. Holding each stuffed crab with tongs, dip into batter. Then place into the deep fryer filled with hot vegetable oil. Completely cover the crab and fry individually for 7 minutes or until golden. To SERVE: Arrange French-fried Jimmy crabs on a serving platter and garnish with lemon wedges. *Serves six.*

Florida Stone Crab

Menippe mercenaria

Approximately 98 percent of the stone crab catch is landed in Florida. The stone crab fishery harvests only the large, meaty claws of the crabs, and the animal is released alive. Stone crabs can regenerate their claws up to four times, and about 10 percent of crab claws seen in Florida packing houses are regrown.

In some areas, the recreational mangrove crab fishery is larger than the commercial fishery. Nevertheless, management imposes bag limits and limits on the number of pots or nets per person or per boat to reduce heavy exploitation by both commercial and recreational fishers.

Adult stone crabs are characterized by their rock-hard shell and two large claws. The body is dark brownish-red mottled with dusky gray. An interesting feature about the stone crab is a mark on each claw that resembles a thumb print.

Stone crabs inhabit bays and estuaries where they hide under rocks and shell fragments. When fully grown, they move into shoals just below the low tide mark and dig burrows in which to live. Stone crabs are found along the Atlantic and Gulf Coasts but are commercially harvested almost entirely in Florida. They feed on small fish, various crustaceans, and clams.

Fishery regulations specify a harvest season of mid-October to mid-May. Stone crabs are captured commercially with traps which are re-baited every other day. Stone crabs are carnivorous and sometimes resort to cannibalism while in traps. In order to assure the continued survival of the species, Florida law forbids the taking of whole stone crabs. Only one claw may be removed so the crab can survive and defend itself, and no claws may be removed from egg bearing females.

Green Mangrove Crab

Scylla serrata

Mangrove crabs, also known as mud or black crabs, are widely distributed throughout the Indo-West Pacific from the east coast of Africa to northern Australia and across the western Pacific to Tahiti. They were introduced to Hawaii more than 55 years ago.

Mangrove crabs commonly inhabit sheltered estuaries, mud flats, mangrove forests, and the tidal reaches of some rivers—although females carrying eggs are present in deeper waters offshore. These crabs favor a soft, muddy bottom, often below the low tide level.

There are two species of mangrove crab— the green and the brown mangrove crab. The green mangrove crab, which is the more desirable, grows larger than the brown and is deep green in color, with paler green mottling on the claws, legs and rear flippers. The green mud crab also has a pair of double spines situated just behind each claw and another pair on each wrist.

Commercially, mangrove crabs are caught in wire mesh pots. Traps are usually set at night from small runabouts. Drop nets are also used. Mangrove crabs are extremely abundant, particularly off Australia's Northern Territory, where they are well regulated by the Department of Fisheries

Seafood WATCH

Although there is concern with the environmental damage caused by the large numbers of crab traps and ropes, the stone crab fishery is considered sustainable. The populations appear to be holding steady, and fishermen and managers have created a plan that will gradually reduce fishing efforts over the next 30 years. Stone crab is a "Best Choice" for consumers.

For current fishery status, visit www.seafoodwatch.org

Seafood WATCH

Based on current reports, mangrove crab are caught in traps, a method considered eco-friendly because fishermen can release undersized crabs and other bycatch unharmed. The Australian mangrove crab fishery is considered well-managed by the states and Northern Territory. Mangrove crab is a "Good Alternative," although it has not yet been evaluated by the Seafood Watch Program.

For current fishery status, visit www.seafoodwatch.org

Curried Florida Stone Crab Claws with Hot Marmalade Dip

FLORIDA DEPARTMENT OF AGRICULTURE, Tallahassee, Florida

✦

2½ to 4 pounds fresh Florida stone crab claws (frozen acceptable) ▪ ½ cup butter, softened ▪ 1 teaspoon curry powder ▪ ⅓ cup orange marmalade ▪ ¼ cup lime juice ▪ ¼ cup soy sauce ▪ 1 clove garlic, minced

Crack and remove out shell from the claws, leaving meat attached to the moveable pincer. Cream together butter and curry powder. Spread curry butter over both sides of stone crab claws and arrange on broiling pan. TO PREPARE THE MARMALADE DIP: Combine remaining ingredients, mixing well. Cook the mixture, stirring constantly, until clear and thickened; keep warm until ready to serve. Place broiler pan with crab claws about 3 inches from heat source and broil 2 to 3 minutes, turning once, or until hot. TO SERVE: Arrange claws on serving platter accompanied with the hot marmalade dip. *Serves four to six.*

Sautéed Mangrove Crab with Cilantro and Sweet Chili Sauce

CHEF MAL STOCKTON, GONE BUSH CAMPING, Darwin, Australia, *in association with* **Gondwana Tours**

✦

4 live mangrove crabs ▪ 3 tablespoons olive oil ▪ 2 cloves garlic, minced ▪ 2 red hot peppers (Thai), diced ▪ ¼ cup fresh cilantro, chopped ▪ ¼ cup bottled sweet chili sauce

Place live crab in boiling salted water and cook for approx. 15 minutes (after the water returns to a boil), turning the shell bright orange. Immerse the cooked crabs in cold water to cool. Clean the crabs by removing and discarding the top shell, gills and viscera. Remove the legs, and break the remaining bodies in half. Heat a wok or skillet to high heat and add the olive oil. Stir fry the crab claws and body halves for 4 to 5 minutes until claws are bright red. Add garlic, red peppers, cilantro, and sweet chili sauce; stir fry another 2 to 3 minutes, stirring frequently. TO SERVE: Arrange the cooked crab on a large serving platter and pour over remaining juice. Garnish with cilantro sprigs, hot peppers, and a top shell from one of the crabs. *Serves four.*

Curried Florida Stone Crab Claws with Hot Marmalade Dip

Pink Shrimp

Pandalus

About three-quarters of world shrimp production is wild-caught, further broken down into 70 percent warmwater and 30 percent coldwater shrimp. The remaining quarter of total production is farm-raised tropical shrimp. With worldwide shrimp fisheries at or near maximum sustainable yield, many nations are turning to farm-raised shrimp as an attractive alternative.

Judging from the enormous amount consumed each year, shrimp has become America's most popular shellfish. Their meaty texture, lack of bones, and ready-to-eat convenience all contribute to their popularity. Among the hundreds of species that inhabit the world's seas is the pink shrimp. Two abundant varieties are the northern pink *(Pandalus borealis)*, which dwells in Alaska's icy cold waters, and the ocean pink *(Pandalus jordani)*, which is caught from central California to Washington State.

Commonly known as "bay shrimp," pink shrimp are small, spindly, long-bodied crustaceans averaging three to five inches in length. They thrive on muddy ocean bottoms where they live on a diet of plankton and krill. These miniature shellfish prefer fairly deep water (180 to 1,200 feet), although most are caught between 360 and 600 feet.

Pink shrimp are trawl-caught using special nets. Although large volumes of shrimp can be caught using this method, there is bycatch involved.

Delivered on ice, pink shrimp are rushed to the processing plant where they are cooked, peeled

Seafood WATCH

U.S. shrimp trawlers outfit their nets with devices to let sea turtles and some fish escape from their nets. U.S. shrimp farmers, meanwhile, are subject to laws limiting environmental impacts as damages can occur. U.S. trap-caught shrimp is the "Best Choice" because this method is a low-bycatch, sustainable alternative. U.S. trawl-caught or farmed shrimp fall under the "Caution" category, while consumers should "Avoid" all imported shrimp—whether it is wild-caught or farmed—due to high bycatch and habitat damage.

For current fishery status, visit www.seafoodwatch.org

and frozen for market. Yields range from 200 to 700 shrimp per pound. Shrimp in counts over 500 (called "pinheads" in the industry) are extremely small and are considered of lower quality. Pink shrimp are usually marketed in one- and five-pound units. Shelf life for fresh shrimp is four to six days. If handled well and protected from freezer burn, frozen shrimp can last one year.

Pink shrimp have a sweet, delicate taste and are generally considered more flavorful than warm water varieties. Live, the tail of the pink shrimp is more red than pink. Cooked, the shell is pink and the meat is an opaque white tinged with pink. The meat is firm and crisp in texture, and moister than tropical shrimp.

❖ ❖ ❖

Shrimp is a fast-selling item, so it is often displayed along side other, slower-moving seafood. Remember that pink shrimp are cooked and ready to eat, so do not let them come into contact with raw seafood or bacterial contamination may result.

Carolina Shrimp Gumbo

Carolina Shrimp Gumbo

CHEF SCOTT LONG, A.W. SHUCKS, Charleston, South Carolina

✦

1 to 1½ pounds medium-cooked and peeled shrimp ▪ 1 pound fresh bay scallops ▪ ½ stick margarine ▪ ¾ cup flour ▪ 1 cup green bell pepper, diced ▪ 1 cup yellow onion, diced ▪ 1 cup celery, diced ▪ 2 to 3 tablespoons Tabasco sauce ▪ ¼ cup Worcestershire ▪ 1½ ounce shrimp bouillon ▪ 1½ ounce ham bouillon ▪ 4 cans diced tomato ▪ 2 cups fresh okra, cut ▪ 1½ cups fresh corn kernels ▪ 1 pound smoked sausage ▪ gumbo filé powder (as needed; approx. ¼ cup) ▪ ¾ gallon cold water ▪ chopped parsley (as needed)

In a medium-size pan, melt margarine and add flour while mixing with whisk to form a roux; reserve. In a large soup pot, sauté peppers, onions, and celery until translucent. Add shrimp, scallops, Tabasco, shrimp and ham bouillon, Worcestershire, corn, okra, diced tomatoes, and water. Cut smoked sausage into bite size coins and add to pot. Simmer for one hour and add the roux. Simmer until roux cooks out (no lumps and gumbo has thickened). Turn off heat and add gumbo filé. Mix thoroughly. Adjust flavor to liking and let sit for 20 to 30 minutes for flavor to come out. NOTE: Gumbo filé will need to be adjusted on a per batch basis and add roux in small amounts to achieve desired consistency. TO SERVE: Ladle into bowls and garnish with fresh chopped parsley. Makes six quarts.

Shrimp and Mango Summer Roll

CHEF ELIAS LOPEZ, ROY'S AT THE INN AT SPANISH BAY, Pebble Beach, California

✦

8 wild-caught shrimp (cooked and sliced in half) ▪ 2 limes, separated into segments ▪ 1 tablespoon fish sauce ▪ 1 tablespoon brown sugar ▪ ¼ pound pea shoots ▪ 16 fresh shiso leaves ▪ 8 round rice paper wrappers (6 to 8-inch) ▪ 1 mango, peeled and sliced ▪ salt and pepper to taste

Combine lime segments, fish sauce and brown sugar; mix well. Add pea shoots, shiso leaves, salt and pepper and toss well; set aside. Soak rice papers in warm water until soft and palatable, then drain on clean dry towel. Place ½ cup of the filling, mango and shrimp on lower third of rice paper; roll as tightly as possible. *Makes eight rolls.*

Alaska Spot Prawn

Pandalus platyceros

For decades, spot prawns have been caught in traps, which seem to have had little impact on their population. But as the demand for spot prawns grows, fishers have begun large-scale harvests using trawl nets, which may both decrease their numbers and damage the habitat where they live.

In the North Pacific waters of Alaska, there are five types of shrimp: Northern Pink, Humpy, Coonstripe, Sidestripe, and Spot shrimp.

Spot shrimp, also known as "spot prawns," are the largest shrimp in Alaska's waters, reaching lengths of ten inches. They range from light brown to orange in color with paired spots on their back just behind their head and just in front of their tail—hence the name spot shrimp.

As part of the *Palandid* family, the spot shrimp changes sex during its lifetime. It spends its early life as a male, then transforms into a female for the remainder of its life.

Spot shrimp are found in the northeastern Pacific Ocean from southern Alaska to southern California and also in Asian waters around the Sea of Japan. They are found on rocky bottoms from intertidal to over 250 fathoms in depth. Spot shrimp forage on the bottom, feeding on other shrimp, plankton, small mollusks, worms, sponges, and fish carcasses.

Alaska's commercial shrimp fisheries use two types of harvesting methods: trawling and pot (trap) fishing. Northern pink, humpy, and sidestripe shrimp are caught using trawlers, while coon-

stripe and spot shrimp are caught using shrimp pots—a more environmentally-friendly way of fishing because it reduces bycatch. The basic shrimp trap is made of mesh or wire and is oblong with a conical entrance at each end. Some gear studies suggest enclosed traps may be more efficient than traps with mesh or wire sides. However, traps with mesh or wire sides allow undersized shrimp to escape.

Spot shrimp, like other varieties of shrimp, are sized and sold by count (number of shrimp per pound), either whole or headless. For example, a 16-20 count of headless shrimp means there are 16 to 20 headless shrimp per pound. Counts for headless shrimp range from under ten (the largest shrimp) to 300-500 (the smallest).

pot shrimp are an excellent source of high-quality protein and are low in fat. Store fresh shrimp

✦ ✦ ✦

S in the refrigerator at 32°-38°F and use within two days, or store in the freezer and use within six months.

Gamberoni alla Toscana

Chef Alfonso Curti, Grappolo's Trattoria, Santa Ynez, California

✦

6 large Alaskan spot prawns ▪ 6 sliced pieces of pancetta (Italian ham) ▪ 12 ounces cannellini beans (cooked in jar) ▪ 2-3 bunches fresh spinach ▪ 2-3 cloves garlic ▪ 2-3 fresh sage leaves ▪ olive oil (as needed) ▪ butter (as needed) ▪ chili flakes (as needed) ▪ fresh parsley (as needed) ▪ 1 lemon ▪ salt and pepper to taste

Wash shrimp with cold water. Remove tail shell and de-vein shrimp. Leave head/body shell intact. Wrap one slice of pancetta around each section of tail meat. Secure with toothpick if necessary. In a hot skillet, add olive oil and butter, and sauté shrimp for 1-2 minutes. Transfer skillet to preheated oven and bake at 450° for 15 minutes. While shrimp are baking, sauté fresh spinach with olive oil and a small pinch or 2 of chopped garlic, salt, pepper, and chili flakes. When leaves become wilted, remove spinach from pan. In another skillet, sauté the cannellini beans with sage, butter, and a small pinch of chili flakes, for 5 minutes. To SERVE: Ladle some beans in center of each plate. Place the sautéed spinach around the beans. Arrange 3 shrimp in a teepee-like fashion in center of dish. Garnish with fresh chopped parsley and lemon wedges. Drizzle some olive oil over shrimp just before serving. *Serves two.*

Stuffed Alaska Spot Prawns

Fisherman's Express, Alaska Seafoods, Anchorage, Alaska

✦

8 jumbo Alaska spot prawns ▪ ¼ pound smoked salmon ▪ 1 tablespoon chopped parsley ▪ 1 tablespoon olive oil ▪ 2 tablespoons minced onions ▪ 2 egg whites ▪ 1 tablespoon minced garlic ▪ ⅓ cup dry white wine ▪ ¼ cup bread crumbs ▪ 3 tablespoons unsalted butter

Peel the prawns. Using a small knife, make a deep slit down the back. Remove and discard the vein and set 6 prawns aside in the refrigerator. Heat the olive oil in a small skillet over medium heat, add the onion and garlic and cook, stirring for about 2 minutes. Remove from heat and scrape into a food processor. Add the bread crumbs, parsley, smoked salmon, 2 leftover prawns, and egg white to the blender and blend until smooth. Scrape the mixture into a small bowl. Remove the prawns from the refrigerator and lay them flat on a work surface. Spoon some stuffing into each prawn and lightly press the sides together around the stuffing. Preheat a broiler. Arrange stuffed prawns in a small ovenproof dish, pour in the wine and place under the broiler for about 4 minutes or until prawns and stuffing are completely opaque in color. To SERVE: Remove prawns from the broiler and transfer them to 2 serving plates. Stir the butter into remaining liquid in the broiling pan and pour over the prawns. *Serves two.*

Gamberoni alla Toscana

California Spiny Lobster

Panulirus interruptus

The California spiny lobster is a small but locally-important commercial fishery based in southern California, as well as a well-established recreational fishery. Based on 83 years of landings data, the lobster population is a healthy fishery with low bycatch and without any damage to the habitat.

Spiny lobster is the general name given to about four dozen species of clawless lobster found throughout the tropical and subtropical waters of the world, as well as in the temperate seas of the Southern Hemisphere. Despite this variety, most are sold under the names warm water lobster (from Florida, California, or Hawaii) or cold water lobster (from Australia or New Zealand).

The California spiny lobster ranges from northern California south to Baja, Mexico. These lobsters are nearly always sold fresh, either live or cooked. In contrast, most Atlantic and Australian caught spiny lobster are only available as frozen raw tails.

California spiny lobsters are commercially caught using baited traps set in shallow, rocky areas. The lobsters hide in rock dens during the day and come out to search for food at night. Lobsters feed on crabs, sea cucumbers, plankton, shrimp, fish, and squid.

When alive, California spiny lobsters are beautifully marked with mottled yellow, orange, green and blue over a predominately rust-colored body. They may grow to twenty pounds, but most commonly are between one and five pounds. Spiny lobsters lack the large claws of their Maine cousins, but more than make up for the absence of this weapon by having large, formidable looking antennae, a shell covered with sharp spines, and a large powerful tail which can be used in defense or for rapid retreat.

The California spiny lobster, like the Australian rock lobster, is abundant because the fishery is well managed. To assure a healthy commercial stock of California spiny lobsters, the Department of Fish & Game enforces strict regulations. Although the California spiny lobster accounts for only about two percent of the total U.S. spiny lobster market, this lobster, and the Australian rock lobster, are the best choices, and should be requested when purchasing or dining out.

✦   ✦   ✦

When buying live lobster, the freshest lobsters are alive and frisky; their tails curl up or flap rather than hang limply down when they are picked up. Ask how long the lobster has been in the tank and choose those that have been there less than a week. The lobster should also seem heavy for its size and the shell should be hard rather than spongy. A soft, spongy shell is the sign of a lobster that has recently shed, which means it will have a very low percentage of meat. If buying cooked lobster, be sure the tail is pulled tightly up underneath the body, which indicates the lobster was alive when cooked. Fresh-cooked lobster should also smell fresh, with no hint of ammonia odor. The shell should be bright orange or red and any exposed meat should be white and moist, not dried out or yellow.

Lobster Tail with Caviar, Seared Shallot Griddlecakes and Chervil Mascarpone

Lobster Tail with Caviar, Seared Shallot Griddlecakes and Chervil Mascarpone

CHEF CHARLES BUTLER, WATERFRONT RESTAURANT, Camden, Maine, *in association with* **Stolt Sea Farm, California**

❖

2 live spiny lobster ▪ 2 tablespoons Mascarpone cheese ▪ 2 tablespoons cream ▪ 1½ teaspoons freshly-chopped chervil ▪ 1 tablespoon vegetable oil ▪ 3 shallots, peeled and sliced ▪ ½ cup all-purpose flour ▪ ½ teaspoon baking powder ▪ ¼ teaspoon salt ▪ ¼ teaspoon ground white pepper ▪ ¼ teaspoon sugar ▪ 1 egg ▪ ⅓ cup milk ▪ mesclun leaves for garnish ▪ ½ ounce caviar

Mix Mascarpone, cream, chervil, and add salt and pepper to taste; set aside. In skillet, heat oil. Add shallots and cook, stirring occasionally until golden. In a bowl, mix flour, baking powder, salt, pepper and sugar. Whisk egg into milk. Pour egg mixture into flour mixture. Stir just until combined. If mixture appears too thick, stir in additional milk. Add shallots. Heat griddle or large skillet to medium-high; lightly brush with oil. Drop 2 to 3 tablespoons batter onto griddle for each griddlecake. Form 6 griddlecakes. Cook on first side until edges begin to dry. Turn, cook on second side for 30 seconds or until golden. In a large pot, boil water with salt if desired. Add lobster and cook for 10 minutes per pound (add 2 minutes for each ¼ pound). Begin timing once the water has returned to a boil. Remove lobster and let cool until easy to handle. Remove tail meat, leaving tail fan intact. For each serving, place 3 griddlecakes, with edges overlapping, in the center of each plate. Top each serving with lobster tail, 2 tablespoons Mascarpone mixture, a few mesclun leaves, and 1 to 2 teaspoons caviar. *Serves two.*

Spiny Lobster with Leek Tartar and Pickled Tomato

CHEF ISABELLE ALEXANDRE, CITRONELLE, Santa Barbara, California

❖

4 live spiny lobsters, 1 to 1½ pounds each ▪ 8 leeks (white and light green parts only) ▪ FOR THE VINAIGRETTE: 1 egg yolk ▪ 1 tablespoon Dijon mustard ▪ 1 tablespoon sherry vinegar ▪ ½ cup olive oil ▪ FOR THE PICKLED TOMATO: 6 red tomatoes ▪ 3 shallots, finely chopped ▪ ¼ cup sherry vinegar ▪ 2 tablespoons granulated sugar ▪ ¼ cup chopped chives for garnish ▪ extra virgin olive oil ▪ salt and pepper to taste

Remove both ends of the leeks and wash well. Cut them in half lengthwise and slice into ¼" pieces. Put in double boiler and steam for 10-15 minutes until soft; reserve. In a large pot, boil water with salt if desired. Add lobster and cook for 5 minutes. Remove lobster and plunge in ice water bath. Remove the tails and cut each tail lengthwise. You can keep the meat in or out of the shell; reserve in refrigerator. Peel tomatoes and finely chop to a pulp. In a bowl, add the tomatoes, shallots, sherry vinegar, and sugar and let marinate for 30 minutes; reserve. In another bowl, prepare the vinaigrette by mixing the egg yolk, mustard, sherry vinegar, and olive oil. Warm the chopped leaks in microwave and toss with the vinaigrette. Remove lobster from refrigerator, baste with olive oil and water, cover and place in 325°F preheated oven for 2-3 minutes. While cooking, spoon ½ cup of the leeks in center of plate. Remove lobster tails and arrange around the leeks. Sprinkle the pickled tomatoes over the lobster. Finish with a drizzle of olive oil and chopped chives around the dish. *Serves four.*

Maine Lobster

Homarus americanus

MAINE LOBSTER

The management of the lobster resource is in transition. The Federal Sustainable Fisheries Act, passed in 1996, identified the resource as being overfished and mandated the rebuilding of the fishery. Today, strong conservation measures are being implemented by the State of Maine and its commercial lobstermen.

Long ago, lobsters were so plentiful that Native Americans used them to fertilize their fields and to bait their hooks for fishing. In colonial times, lobsters were considered "poverty food." They were harvested from tidal pools and served to children, servants, and prisoners.

Today, Maine lobster, also called the American lobster, remains on the menu—but as a high-priced delicacy.

The Maine lobster is known for its two large claws: a big-toothed crusher claw for pulverizing shells and a finer-edged ripper claw resembling a steak knife, for tearing soft flesh.

Maine lobsters can survive on all types of ocean bottoms but prefer a rocky or muddy substrate. Their range extends along the northeast Atlantic coasts of Canada and the United States, with the largest populations located in the Gulf of Maine. Maine lobsters are aggressive and will fight for possession of rocky cave shelters. They are scavengers, taking what food comes to them. Not especially skilled hunters, most lobsters feed on carrion, clams, snails, mussels, worms, and sea urchins. If desperate for food, lobster will eat another of its kind. Because of this natural cannibalistic nature, fishermen band their claws together when they are caught.

The color of the Maine lobster is usually olive green or greenish brown, though dusky orange and even bright blue lobsters are sometimes found. Diet, heredity, and exposure to light all affect a lobster's color. The major pigment in a lobster's shell is actually bright red in its free state, but in the lobster's shell it is chemically bound to proteins that change it to a greenish or bluish color. When lobsters are cooked, heat breaks down these bonds, freeing the pigment so that it reverts to its normal red color.

❖ ❖ ❖

Maine lobsters are caught using traps baited with fish. They have been harvested commercially since the mid 1800s. Before this time, lobsters were very large in population, bigger in size and lived much longer. Despite heavy fishing today, these lobsters continue to thrive. Thanks in part to overfishing laws, particularly in Maine, female lobsters carrying eggs are released back into the water, helping the lobster population to increase. Maine is also the only state where it is illegal to catch lobster under one pound and over four pounds. When selecting Maine lobster, ask questions to make sure what you are buying is, in fact, a Maine lobster and not one from another state or Canada.

Maine Lobster and Avocado Salad with Red Wine Marinated Onion, Lemon Mayonnaise and Field Greens

CHEFS MARK GAIER & CLARK FRAISER, ARROWS RESTAURANT, Ogunquit, Maine

◆

2 live Maine lobsters (1¼ pounds each) ▪ 2 ripe avocados ▪ ½ cup mayonnaise ▪ ½ lemon, cut in sections ▪ ¼ pound mixed field greens ▪ 1 grapefruit, sectioned ▪ 1 large red onion, cut into ⅛-inch rounds ▪ FOR THE MARINADE: ¼ cup red wine vinegar ▪ ½ cup olive oil ▪ 1 tablespoon peppercorns ▪ 2 sprigs fresh tarragon ▪ 2 sprigs thyme ▪ 1 teaspoon kosher salt ▪ FOR THE VINAIGRETTE: ¼ cup champagne vinegar ▪ ¼ cup olive oil ▪ ¼ cup extra virgin olive oil ▪ salt and pepper to taste

Bring a pot of hot salted water to a boil. Place the lobsters in the pot and cook for 12 minutes. Carefully pour out into a colander and immediately ice lobsters. When the lobsters are cool, pick and set aside in the refrigerator. In a stainless saucepan, bring all the marinade ingredients to a boil. Slice onions and place on a cookie sheet. Pour marinade over the onions and cool in the refrigerator. Place vinegar, salt and pepper in a bowl and whisk in the olive oil and extra virgin olive oil; reserve. Wash and dry the field greens, wrap in a clean towel, and refrigerate. Thinly slice avocados and place on 4 chilled plates. TO SERVE: Place onions around the edge of the plate. Toss the field greens with champagne vinaigrette and place on plates. Slice the lobster tails into six medallions and place around each plate. Garnish with grapefruit sections. Drizzle remaining vinaigrette over the avocado and place a dollop of mayonnaise on each avocado. Serve immediately. *Serves two.*

Saffron Lobster Ramekins

CHEF MARGO BARTELHO, Biddeford, Maine, *First Place Winner - 2004 Maine Lobster Festival Cooking Contest*

◆

1½ pounds cooked lobster meat ▪ 1 shallot ▪ 1 teaspoon dry mustard ▪ ¼ cup garlic ▪ ¾ cup sherry ▪ ½ cup fresh parsley ▪ 1 cup portobella mushrooms ▪ ½ pound unsalted butter ▪ 4 cups heavy cream ▪ 2 egg yolks ▪ 1 tablespoon Old Bay seasoning ▪ ½ pound Monterey Jack cheese ▪ 1 tablespoon sea salt ▪ few threads saffron ▪ 1 teaspoon white pepper ▪ puff pastry sheets

Chop shallot, garlic, mushrooms, and parsley. Grate cheese. Chunk lobster meat and lightly rub with Old Bay, mustard, salt and pepper. Let stand. Melt butter and sauté shallot, garlic, mushrooms, and parsley until shallots and garlic are transparent and the mushrooms are browned. Add lobster meat to the sauté pan, then add the sherry and cook down. Remove from heat and let stand, stirring occasionally. In a small pot, heat the cream. Temper egg yolks with the cream and whisk. Add few threads finely-crushed saffron, and reduce cream to half. After cream has fully reduced, whisk in grated cheese until melted. Remove from heat and fold cream mixture into lobster mixture. Fill individual ramekins with mixture to the top. Cut the puff pastry to fit the ramekin tops, and brush with egg wash. Bake at 350°F until tops are browned and bubbly. *Serves four to six.*

Maine Lobster and Avocado Salad with Red Wine Marinated Onion, Lemon Mayonnaise and Field Greens

MOLLUSKS & OTHER

Red Abalone

Haliotis rufescens

Due to a rapid decline in the coastal wild abalone population, commercial abalone diving is illegal in U.S. waters. Aquaculture facilities such as the Abalone Farm in Cayucos, California, offer a legal and sustainable source for this product.

Abalone are marine snails, with some 70 modern species occurring globally. Abalone fossils have been found in rocks dating from as much as 70 million years ago. They are a relative of clams, scallops, octopi, and squid.

In North America, abalone is native only on the Pacific Coast, from Alaska to the Baja Peninsula in Mexico.

Each abalone possesses an external top shell and a large muscular "foot" for attaching itself to a rock surface and sometimes for locomotion, although a mature abalone generally resides in one spot. Abalone feed exclusively on algae and kelp.

Black abalone live in tidal pools from Oregon to the southern tip of Baja, Mexico. Green abalone, pink abalone, and white abalone prefer southern climes, with each species occupying increasingly deeper waters, respectively. Red abalone, the largest species, occupies tidal pools in Oregon to deep reefs as far south as Baja. The red or coral color of the outer surface of a red abalone shell results from consumption of red algae.

Humans have utilized abalone for food, tools, and jewelry for millennia. Five of the eight eastern Pacific abalones were abundant enough to support multimillion-dollar fisheries through most of the twentieth century. Nearly all of the abalone consumed in the United States was harvested in California. By the late 1900s, the commercial abalone landing declined and annual harvests continued to exceed the rate of re-population for all species, resulting in a dramatic decline in the abalone fishery.

✦ ✦ ✦

Today, with the worldwide supply of wild abalone still in decline, the industry has turned to aquaculture, the cultivation of abalone in aquatic farms. Farmed abalone is available live or as cleaned whole meat medallions and tenderized steaks. Presently, there are 13 abalone farms operating in California to meet the demand for this luxury seafood. The Abalone Farm in Cayucos, California is the oldest and largest producer of farm-raised abalone in the United States.

Seafood WATCH

Depletion of wild populations has encouraged the farming of abalone in many countries to meet the demand for this luxury seafood. In California, farm-raised abalone are harvested when their shells are no more than four inches long, so any abalone bigger than that is probably "poached," or sold illegally by a sport diver. Farmed abalone is a "Best Choice."

For current fishery status, visit www.seafoodwatch.org

Sesame Mint Abalone in Lemon Shells

CHEF FORREST COOK, COSTANOA COASTAL LODGE AND CAMP, Pescadero, California

◆

½ pound fresh farmed abalone ▪ 1 medium cucumber ▪ 4 lemons ▪ 2 tablespoons seasoned rice vinegar ▪ 1 tablespoon sugar ▪ 4 red radishes ▪ a few leaves of fresh mint ▪ 1 teaspoon toasted sesame seeds ▪ 1 cup white wine ▪ 1 teaspoon garlic, minced ▪ pinch of sea salt

For tender abalone, it is important that the abalone be fresh and cleaned quickly after purchase. Shell and wash abalone. Place meat in a kitchen towel and pound with a cook's mallet until abalone is about ¼-inch thick. Large abalone should be butterfly sliced before pounding. Reserve in a covered bowl in refrigerator. Cut lemons in half, and also cut a small slice from each tip end so lemon halves can sit upright. Core lemons using a sharp-sided spoon. Save the juice. Peel cucumber, cut in half lengthwise and core out seeds with a small spoon. Slice cucumber into ¼-inch-thick half moons and place in a small bowl. Add rice vinegar, 4 tablespoons lemon juice, sugar, and a pinch of salt and toss. FOR THE ABALONE: In a small saucepan, heat white wine, garlic, and ¼ cup lemon juice to a boil. Poach abalone in hot wine mixture for only 40 seconds, then plunge cooked abalone into a small ice bath and quickly drain. Slice cooked abalone into ¼-inch-thick strips. TO SERVE: Combine abalone with cucumber mixture and spoon into the lemon cups. Garnish with thin slices of radish and sprinkle sesame seeds on top. *Serves four to eight.*

Abalone in Beurre Blanc with Tea-Steeped Raisins and Toasted Almonds

CHEF BILL HOPPE, HOPPE'S GARDEN BISTRO, Cayucos, California

◆

18 abalone steaks (pounded) ▪ 3 lemons ▪ 6 eggs, lightly beaten ▪ 2 cups flour, sifted ▪ salt to taste ▪ FOR THE BEURRE BLANC SAUCE: 1 cup dry white wine ▪ 2 tablespoons champagne vinegar ▪ 2 shallots, chopped ▪ ¼ cup crème fraîche ▪ 12 tablespoons sweet butter ▪ salt and white pepper to taste ▪ FOR THE TEA-STEEPED RAISINS: ¼ cup dark raisins or currants ▪ strongly-brewed black tea (enough to cover raisins) ▪ 4 ounces slivered almonds (toasted until golden brown in 375°F oven; approx. 10 minutes)

Brew tea and pour over raisins. Let the raisins soak until they swell (approx. 2 hours). Drain off any excess liquid; reserve. Prepare Beurre Blanc Sauce by combining wine, vinegar and shallots in a medium saucepan and bring them to a boil. Cook at low rolling boil until liquid has reduced to ¼ cup (approx. 15 minutes). Add crème fraîche and boil until the liquid reduces to ⅓ cup. With a wire whisk, briskly whisk in the small pieces of butter until fully incorporated. Add the tea-steeped raisins and toasted almonds. Season the sauce with salt and white pepper. Strain and keep warm. Season abalone steaks with lemon juice and salt. Dredge through flour and pat off any excess. Dip the seasoned and floured abalone steaks in the beaten eggs, being careful to coat them completely. Sauté very quickly (approx. 5 to 10 seconds on each side) in smoking-hot clarified butter. Place abalone on paper towels to absorb any excess butter. TO SERVE: Laddle Beurre Blanc Sauce on 6 plates. Place 3 cooked abalone steaks on each plate. Garnish with wild rice and snow peas, if desired. *Serves six.*

Sesame Mint Abalone in Lemon Shells

Clams

Because of their sedentary nature, clams are highly susceptible to human-induced changes in their environment. Sewage, agricultural runoff, or other pollution can render shellfish unfit for market. Many shellfish farms, which depend on and use clean water, provide a better alternative than some "wild" stocks.

Clams are soft-bodied animals that live in shells. The early settlers in North America loved clams and ate them raw, baked, steamed, or chopped in chowder. Clams have a mild, briny taste and a more or less chewy texture, depending on size and variety.

Abundant varieties of clams can be found along beaches in the United States. The four main kinds of Atlantic clams include: hard-shell, soft-shell, surf, and razor. Hard-shell clams (also called quahogs) are usually sold by size. The smallest hardshells are the tender and sweet littlenecks, which have shells measuring less than two inches across and are often eaten raw or steamed. A little larger are

the cherry stones, which are also quite tender. The largest hardshells, called chowder and mahogany clams, are often chopped and made into soup.

Despite their name, soft-shell clams (also called steamers, fryers, and long necks) have hard, thin shells with neck-like siphons sticking out of them. Surf clams have large, white shells and are usually cut into strips for restaurant use. Razor clams are large, tough clams with shells shaped like straight razors.

Pacific clams include: Pacific littlenecks, Manila clams, geoducks, butter clams, and jackknife clams. Pacific littlenecks (not to be confused with Atlantic littlenecks) are small clams suitable for steaming. Manila (Japanese) clams, introduced from Asia, are good steamed or raw. Geoducks (pronounced "gooey-ducks") are giant Pacific Northwest clams with siphons that may protrude as much as three feet. Butter clams, also native to the Pacific Northwest, are small clams enjoyed raw, steamed, or in stuffing. Western jackknife clams are similar to East Coast razor clams.

Due to increased fishing and various environmental hazards, many kinds of clams are now being farmed, offering a better alternative to wild-caught clams.

❖ ❖ ❖

Farmed clams start out at a hatchery where they are fed continuously and grow rapidly. Once the clams grow to sufficient size, they are taken out to floating nursery rafts. After they grow further, they are shipped to another growing area where they are planted with net panels. The clams work their way through the mesh of the net and into the sand where they are protected from predators. Once they reach market size, the clams are dug and bagged just like in the wild, and suspended from wet storage rafts to purge the sand until they are sold.

Linguine alle Vongole

Linguine alle Vongole

CHEF TONY PERIQUITO, PORTOBELLO YACHT CLUB, Pleasure Island, Disneyworld, Florida, *in association with* **Penn Cove Shellfish, LLC**

◆

40 live steamer clams ▪ 1 pound cooked linguine pasta (according to directions on package) ▪ 2 tablespoons extra virgin olive oil ▪ 6 tablespoons butter ▪ 2 tablespoons fresh Italian parsley, chopped ▪ ½ cup white wine ▪ 1 tablespoon anchovy purée ▪ 2 cloves garlic, chopped ▪ 1 cup chicken or fish stock ▪ 16 cherry tomatoes, cut in half ▪ salt and black pepper to taste

Heat olive oil in a large sauté pan. Add garlic and clams and cook until garlic starts to turn light brown. Add wine, stock, anchovy purée, and butter. Add cooked linguine, tossing constantly until sauce starts to reduce and clams start to open (discard any unopened clams). Add cherry tomatoes, parsley, and salt and pepper to taste. TO SERVE: Place pasta in serving bowls and arrange clams over and around the pasta. *Serves four to six.*

Pacific Littleneck Clams in Butter and White Wine

CHEF CYNTHIA MARIE ANDERSON, Eugene, Oregon

◆

3 pounds fresh littleneck clams (washed thoroughly) ▪ 2 strips bacon, diced ▪ 1 stalk celery, diced ▪ 2 or 3 cloves garlic, minced ▪ 4 tablespoons butter ▪ 1 lemon, juiced ▪ freshly grated Parmesan cheese (as needed) ▪ Italian parsley, chopped (as needed) ▪ 1 small pinch cayenne pepper ▪ 1 cup chicken stock ▪ 1 cup dry white wine ▪ ¼ cup fresh herbs (basil or thyme) ▪ 1 tomato, chopped ▪ sea salt and cracked pepper to taste

In a large pot, melt butter over medium heat. Add diced bacon and celery. Cook until celery is translucent and bacon is cooked through. Add lemon juice, wine, and chicken stock until liquid is 1½" deep (add additional wine if necessary). Bring liquid to a soft boil. Next, add garlic, fresh herbs, cayenne pepper, salt and pepper, and clams. Cover and steam (approx. 2 to 3 minutes or until clams have opened; do not overcook). Remove pot from heat and add the chopped tomato. TO SERVE: Ladle clams with the nectar into individual serving bowls (discard any unopened clams). Top with freshly grated Parmesan cheese and parsley. Accompany with fresh baked sourdough bread. *Serves four.*

Blue Mussels

Mytilus edulis

BLUE MUSSELS

Mussel farming is not only well developed in the United States, but in New Zealand as well. New Zealanders went through a fishery collapse and developed the mussel culture as a better alternative. Today, mussel growers work to protect the environment while their mussel leases are managed for sustainability.

Blue mussels are slender black bivalve mollusks with a blue inner shell. They live attached to rocks and other hard surfaces along coastal areas in many parts of the world. Off North America, they occur on both the West and East coasts.

Mussels are highly efficient feeders. They can filter ten to 15 gallons of water a day, consuming virtually everything in it.

A longtime favorite delicacy in Europe, mussels are gaining popularity in the United States. Their flavored but somewhat chewy flesh ranges from cream to orange in color. As demand increases, wild

populations must be supplemented by aquaculture so that depletion of natural beds does not occur. In the United States, successful commercial farms exist in Maine, Massachusetts, Rhode Island, and Washington State. Mussels are cultured by three basic methods: rope culture (plastic ropes or mesh tubes hanging from rafts), bouchot culture (using posts instead of ropes), and beach culture (bottom culture).

The Penn Cove Shellfish Company located in Washington State is America's oldest and largest commercial mussel farm. They farm the world-famous Penn Cove mussel *(Mytilus trossulus)*, which has won numerous international mussel taste contests. In the wild, Penn Cove mussels range from Alaska to Washington, preferring pristine bays where snowmelt keeps the salinity lower than the open ocean. Penn Cove mussels are mild in texture, full of sweet flavor, and are grown to a market size of two-and-one-half to three inches in one year.

Another common farmed blue mussel is the Mediterranean mussel *(Mytilus galloprovencialis)*. Unique in appearance and flavor, they are known as the Mediterranean mussel because they are farmed in southern France, Spain, Italy, and Greece. Mediterranean mussels do occur naturally in a few bays of Washington State and are now farmed in select bays throughout the Northwest. Mediterranean mussels will grow to a larger size, making them great for serving stuffed, smoked or marinated.

✦ ✦ ✦

Farmed mussels are sold live, frozen whole, as frozen or canned meat, and sometimes smoked. It is easy to tell the difference between farmed and wild mussels in that the shells of wild mussels are rough, while farm-raised mussels have a clean, smooth shell.

Curried Mussels

KASPAR'S RESTAURANT, Seattle, Washington, *in association with* **Penn Cove Shellfish, LLC**

◆

1½ pounds live mussels, debearded ▪ 1 cup dry white wine ▪ 1 cup heavy cream ▪ 2 cloves garlic, minced ▪ 1 tablespoon shallot, minced ▪ 1 stalk lemongrass (lower 6 inches only), outer leaves discarded and root end trimmed, cut into 1-inch pieces ▪ 2 teaspoons curry powder ▪ 1 tablespoon scallion, thinly sliced ▪ 1 tablespoon unsalted butter

In a large kettle, bring wine and cream to a boil with garlic, shallot, lemongrass and curry powder. Add mussels and cook, covered, over moderately-high heat for 4 to 6 minutes, or until opened. Remove mussels and discard any unopened mussels along with lemongrass. Add to liquid remaining in kettle, scallions, butter, and salt and pepper to taste. Stir until butter is incorporated. TO SERVE: Using a slotted spoon, divide mussels among 4 serving bowls. Spoon the curry sauce over the mussels. *Serves four.*

Mussels with Spicy Tomato and Chili Sauce

HOTEL D'URVILLE IN BLENHEIM, Blenheim, New Zealand, *in association with the* **Penn Cove Shellfish Company, Coupeville, Washington**

◆

2 tablespoons vegetable oil ▪ 1 onion, chopped ▪ ¼ cup tomato paste ▪ 3 tablespoons black bean garlic sauce (available at Asian markets and in the Asian foods section of some supermarkets) ▪ 3 tablespoons jalapeño chilies, minced and seeded ▪ 1 14.5-ounce can diced tomatoes with juice ▪ 1 cup fish stock or bottled clam juice ▪ 2 pounds mussels, scrubbed and debearded

Heat oil in heavy large pot over medium-high heat. Add onion and sauté 5 minutes. Mix in tomato paste, black bean sauce and jalapeños, then tomatoes and fish stock. Bring to a boil. Add the mussels. Cover until mussels open, about 6 minutes (discard any mussels that do not open). TO SERVE: Ladle mussels and tomato mixture into individual serving bowls and serve immediately. *Serves two to four.*

Curried Mussels

West Coast Oysters

Crassostrea gigas

Oyster farming is not only a better alternative than wild-caught oysters, but it has beneficial impacts on local ecosystems. For instance, oysters and their culture structures create valuable habitats for many fish and other marine organisms.

Oysters have lived in the seas for millions of years. Some oyster beds have been dated as far back as the Cretaceous Period, which was more than 65 million years ago. These mollusks also have had a long culinary history. Two thousand years ago, the Romans enjoyed oysters so much that they imported them from all over the Empire. These delicious shellfish haven't lost their popularity since.

Oysters are large shellfish with rough, fluted shells and a creamy-white flesh that has a unique dusky flavor. Oysters grow wild wherever there is firm footing to support their weight. Oyster beds can be found in colonies between tide lines in marsh creeks, flats, and dock pilings.

In today's market, more and more oysters are being grown by aquaculturists on strings or nets, relieving the pressure on wild oyster populations. Companies like Penn Cove Shellfish in Washington State strive to provide the finest in sustainable, farmed shellfish.

Eastern oysters, grown along the Atlantic Coast from Nova Scotia to Florida, are small and have a relatively smooth shell and a mild taste. The Pacific oyster, a briny-tasting delicacy introduced from Japan in the 1920s, ranges in size from the tiny Kumamoto oyster to the large, heavy-shelled Pacific oyster. Olympia oysters are a rare, slow-growing species native to the Pacific Coast. Flat oysters, natives of Europe, are grown in cold waters on both coasts of the United States. They have an intense yet delicate taste.

There are four main types of oyster farming in North America. The traditional bed or bottom culture allows oysters to grow on the grounds of intertidal regions and to feed on the plankton available in the incoming tide. Rack and bag culture consists of cultivating oysters in plastic net bags so water can flow around the oysters, allowing them to continually feed while being protected from predators. Suspended culture is a method of growing oysters in deeper, sub tidal waters. Intertidal longline culture uses 300-600ft ropes containing oysters that are suspended above the natural bed of the intertidal region, which allows oysters to grow faster than they would if settled down into the mud or sand.

✦ ✦ ✦

Farmed oysters can be bought live in the shell or shucked fresh, previously frozen, or smoked. Oysters get their specific tastes from the areas where they are grown, and they are often sold under these place names.

Chilled Oysters with Roasted Poblano-Tequila Mignonette with Avocado-Cilantro Crema

Chilled Oysters with Roasted Poblano-Tequila Mignonette with Avocado-Cilantro Crema

CHEF ANN COOPER, THE ROSS SCHOOL, East Hampton, New York

◆

12 live oysters, scrubbed ▪ 1 fresh poblano chile ▪ 1 small red onion ▪ 3 ounces tequila ▪ 1 ounce fresh lime juice ▪ 1 tablespoon chopped Italian parsley ▪ ½ ripe avocado ▪ 3 tablespoons cilantro leaves ▪ ½ cup sour cream ▪ salt and pepper as needed ▪ juice of 1 lime

Roast the poblano over an open flame or under a broiler until charred. Put in a bowl and cover with a towel to steam slightly and to loosen skin. Remove the charred skin with fingers, and not under running water. Remove the seeds and stem. Dip quickly into cool water to rinse off remaining charred bits; reserve. Medium dice the chile; reserve. Peel and finely dice the red onion. Finely chop the parsley. Mix the tequila, lime juice, chile, onion, and parsley together and let stand for 5 minutes. Add a dash of salt and pepper and taste the mixture. Adjust the salt and lime as needed. In a food processor or blender, combine the avocado, juice of 1 lime, chopped cilantro leaves, sour cream, and salt and pepper. Purée until smooth. Taste and adjust the seasoning as needed. TO SERVE: Shuck the oysters. Top with the tequila mignonette and a dollop of the Avocado-Cilantro Crema. *Serves four.*

Bloody Mary Oysters

OYSTER FARMERS ASSOCIATION OF NSW LTD, TURRAMURRA, New South Wales, Australia

◆

6 fresh oysters in their shells ▪ 1 tablespoon fresh cilantro, finely chopped ▪ 6 ounces tomato juice ▪ 1 tomato, finely diced ▪ 1 red chili, finely chopped ▪ ½ cucumber, peeled, seeded and finely chopped ▪ 1 tablespoon fresh lime juice ▪ splash of vodka ▪ splash of Tabasco sauce ▪ splash of Worcestershire sauce ▪ salt to taste

In a small bowl, toss all the ingredients together, except the oysters. Let Bloody Mary salsa sit for at least an hour, chilled. To SERVE: Shuck the oysters and arrange on a serving plate. Top each freshly opened oyster with a spoonful of Bloody Mary salsa. Return to refrigerator for 30 minutes prior to serving. *Serves two.*

Atlantic Bay Scallop

Aequipecten irradians concentricus

ATLANTIC BAY SCALLOP

Atlantic bay scallops are the most important scallop species fished commercially on the East Coast. Once extensively gathered, the Atlantic bay scallop has become scarce because of overfishing and because eelgrass, which is an important element in its habitat, is largely disappearing. Fortunately, Atlantic bay scallops are now being commercially farmed in the United States.

The scallop is a bivalve meaning it has two shells, also called "valves." Unlike other bivalves such as the clam, scallops do not burrow in the sand. Instead, they lie on the bottom and move by using their adductor muscle to rapidly open and close their valves, propelling them through the water. The adductor muscle, inside and near the edge, is the part that is usually eaten by humans.

The Atlantic bay scallop is found along the southern Atlantic coast, generally in shallow waters where eelgrass is present.

Atlantic bay scallop shells usually have about 17 to 20 ribs and (if they haven't broken off) a pair of "ears" at the hinge. They come in a variety of colors but most are white to dark gray or brown, often with concentric color bands or radial rays of color along the ribs.

Around the edge of the scallop's mantle (the layer of tissue around the scallop's body that secretes the shell) is a series of blue eyes that, though rather weak, can detect movement nearby and warn of the presence of predators, particularly sea stars.

Bay scallops are harvested using dredges, trawls, dip nets, or by hand from shores and bays, particularly around Nantucket and Cape Cod. Where available, farmed bay scallops or scallops caught by professional divers, are much better alternatives than dredge-caught scallops, since such collection methods do not damage the environment. Most of the bay scallops sold in the United States. today are farm-raised.

✦　✦　✦

In general, scallops are often shucked and rushed fresh to processing plants, where they are packed into bags. Bay scallops, which have a sweet and mild flavor, should be purchased fresh—not frozen— to ensure that they remain plump and juicy.

New Bedford, Massachusetts, known as the "Scallop Capitol of the World," is one of the few towns on the Eastern Seaboard where scallops are prevalent. This historic community has held a daily seafood auction since the nineteenth century when young Herman Melville shipped out searching for whales. Seafood distributors like Farm 2 Market get their scallops from this market and ship the scallops live to consumers around the country.

Coquille St. Jacques Montell

TAYLOR SEAFOOD COMPANY, Fairhaven, Massachusetts

✦

12 live bay scallops in shell ▪ 1 tablespoon butter ▪ 1 cup chopped porcini mushrooms ▪ ½ cup shallots ▪ 1 or 2 cloves garlic, chopped ▪ ½ pint heavy cream ▪ ½ cup white wine

In a large sauté pan or shallow pot, sauté butter, mushrooms, shallots, and garlic for several minutes. Add wine, cream, and the live scallops. Sauté for 5 to 6 minutes, or until scallops open.

TO SERVE: Remove scallops from pan and place in a large serving bowl. Pour over remaining scallop broth. *Serves one or two.*

Live Atlantic Bay Scallops with Tarragon Butter

CHEF NANCY CAPUTI , ROSCOE, NEW YORK, *in association with* **Farm 2 Market, New York**

✦

2 dozen live bay scallops ▪ 2 tablespoons unsalted butter ▪ 1 tablespoon fresh tarragon, minced (or 1 teaspoon dried) ▪ 2 teaspoons fresh lemon juice

Start an outdoor grill and get it hot. On a large sheet of heavy aluminum foil, place the scallops (in their shells), along with the butter, tarragon, and lemon juice. Seal firmly and place foil pouch on the grill. Cook until all the scallops are opened (approx. 15 minutes). TO SERVE: Transfer the scallops to a large serving dish and drizzle the "ready-made" sauce in the foil over the scallops. *Serves four.*

Coquille St. Jacques Montell

Atlantic Sea Scallop

Placopecten magellanicus

The commercial fishery for sea scallops occurs year round, and is conducted using primarily dredges and otter trawls. In order to rebuild the sea scallop population and protect the environment, the National Marine Fisheries Service, along with the New England Fishery Management Council's Fishery Management Plan for Atlantic Sea Scallops, institutes day-at-sea restrictions and area closures.

Sea scallops are also known in some areas as giant scallops or the "King of Scallops." Both shells are round, are almost equal in diameter, and are held together by a small, straight hinge and the adductor muscle. The lower shell or valve is white or cream in color and the upper is usually reddish. Inside these shells is the adductor muscle, which is the part of the scallop commonly eaten. Like bay scallops, sea scallops swim through the water by clapping their two shells together.

The most common sea scallop in North American markets, and the one which sets the standard for flavor, is the Atlantic sea scallop. It is a large variety found in relatively deep water of the North Atlantic continental shelf. They range from Newfoundland to North Carolina.

The commercial fishery for Atlantic sea scallops occurs year round, and is conducted using primarily dredges and otter trawls. Despite the methods of harvesting, the U.S. scallop fishery is well managed by the New England Fishery Management Council's Fishery Management Plan for Atlantic Sea Scallops. Management measures include a moratorium on permits, days-at-sea restrictions, closed areas, and restrictions on gear and crew size.

Like the bay scallops, Atlantic seas scallops are shipped all over North America, both frozen and fresh. Buyers on the West Coast, however, may also encounter another large variety which comes from Alaskan waters, the weathervane scallop *(Patinopecten caurinus)*. Although these scallops are especially large, the overall catch is small—only a tiny fraction of the total North American harvest. Because of the distance from the fishing grounds to distribution points and final markets, virtually all of the Alaska scallop catch is frozen at sea.

✦ ✦ ✦

When shopping for fresh or thawed scallops, look for ivory or cream-colored meats, even as dark as a light tan; a stark, bleached white can be a sign of heavy phosphate treatment. There should be little or no milky liquid in the tray. The best dry-packed scallops are often a bit sticky. A fairly strong, sweet-briny aroma is not a problem, but a fishy or sour smell indicates spoilage.

One of the best ways to treat large scallops is like little filet mignons—seared in a hot skillet until the outside is browned and a little crusty and the center is anywhere from rare to medium rare. In company with a substantial side dish, three large sea scallops or four slightly smaller scallops make an adequate portion.

Maine Sea Scallop Carpaccio

Maine Sea Scallop Carpaccio

CHEF ROBERT EVANS, HUGO'S, Portland, Maine

◆

4 fresh jumbo sea scallops, thinly sliced (about 8 slices) ▪ juice of two oranges, strained ▪ 2 teaspoons rice wine vinegar ▪ ½ teaspoon Dijon mustard ▪ pinch of sugar ▪ 1 medium-size egg ▪ ¼ cup canola oil ▪ ⅓ cup extra virgin olive oil ▪ 1 small pink grapefruit, segmented ▪ ¼ cup small capers ▪ ½ cup canola oil for deep frying ▪ coarse kosher sea salt ▪ white pepper ▪ fresh mint and tarragon leaves, julienne

To PREPARE ORANGE EMULSION: Reduce orange juice slowly in heavy bottom pan to ¼-inch. Soft poach the egg and drain. In the blender, place orange juice, poached egg, mustard, vinegar, and sugar. Blend on medium speed until smooth. Continue blending and drizzle canola and olive oil slowly until emulsified. Add salt and pepper to taste. FOR THE FRIED CAPERS: Heat canola oil to 325°F and deep fry until capers blossom and slightly brown. Carefully transfer onto paper towel and drain. TO SERVE: Gently warm sauce in pan. Do not boil. Arrange sliced scallop on cold plates. Place 2 tablespoons of sauce over scallops. Garnish with pink grapefruit segments, fried capers, tarragon, and mint leaves. *Serves one or two.*

Grilled Sea Scallops with Romesco Sauce and Catalan Spinach

CHEF DUNCAN BOYD, VICTORY 96, Portsmouth, New Hampshire

◆

12 to 16 fresh sea scallops (depending on size) muscles removed ▪ 1 tablespoon grape seed oil ▪ FOR THE ROMESCO SAUCE: 1 tablespoon ancho chili powder ▪ 1 tablespoon paprika ▪ 2 whole canned tomatoes, seeds and juice squeezed out ▪ 2 roasted red peppers, stems, skins, and seeds removed ▪ 1 cup almonds ▪ 1 tablespoon chopped fresh garlic ▪ 4 tablespoons sherry vinegar ▪ ½ tablespoon olive oil ▪ 2 tablespoons chopped flat leaf parsley ▪ 2 tablespoons chopped mint ▪ FOR THE CATALAN SPINACH: 1½ pounds baby spinach, cleaned ▪ 2 tablespoons pine nuts ▪ ½ cup golden raisins ▪ ½ cup granny smith apple, peeled and cut into ¼-inch dice ▪ 2 tablespoons olive oil

Prepare the Romesco Sauce by placing chili powder, paprika, tomatoes, almonds, red peppers and garlic in food processor; run for 30 seconds until everything is finely chopped. Add vinegar, parsley, mint, olive oil, and salt and pepper. Pulse again and taste, adding more seasoning, oil or vinegar to taste; set aside. In a large sauté pan over low heat, add olive oil and pine nuts, and cook until nuts begin to color. Add raisins and apple, and sauté for 3 minutes. Add spinach and 2 tablespoons water. Continue to cook until spinach is fully wilted. Season with salt and pepper; set aside and keep warm. Season scallops with salt and pepper, and grill scallops on open flame for 2 minutes. Flip and grill for 1 more minute. NOTE: It may be easier to handle scallops if you skewer them in sets of 4 on bamboo skewers; use 2 skewers per set. TO SERVE: Place a mound of spinach mixture on each plate, place scallops next to spinach and top with Romesco Sauce. *Serves four.*

Market Squid

Loligo opalescens

Bycatch in the squid fishery is considered to be low because seine nets are set on tight schools of squid near surface waters and few other species are captured. The effect of such nets on marine ecosystems is also minimal because the fishing gear rarely interacts with the ocean floor.

In North America, market squid are found in near-shore waters from Baja, California, to southeastern Alaska, although the greatest fishery for this species is off Central and Southern California. Compared to other squid, market squid are relatively small, averaging seven to 12 inches in length.

The squid, like the octopus and nautilus, is a cephalopod—an ancient and specialized group of mollusks. They are considered to be very advanced animals with elaborate sense organs, large brains, and complex behavior. In these respects, cephalopods depart significantly from commonly thought-of mollusks such as snails or clams. Many experts consider a squid's life history and behavior to be more like that of a fish than a mollusk.

Seafood WATCH

As the largest West Coast fishery, California market squid appear to be abundant throughout their range. However, a thorough survey of the population has not been conducted and therefore the stock status remains highly uncertain. Until a management plan is in place to "maintain this fishery at a sustainable level," California market squid move from a "Best Choice" to a "Good Alternatives."

For current fishery status, visit www.seafoodwatch.org

Squids are cigar-shaped with two triangular fins, eight arms, and two feeding tentacles. The squid's effectiveness as a predator is enormously enhanced by its ability to swim rapidly. Once the prey is caught and subdued, the squid's horny beak chops the prey into bite-size pieces. Squid identify their prey visually and so feed best when light is available. Their food is mostly crustaceans, fish, and marine worms. Squid are voracious feeders, capable of consuming 14 percent of their total body weight daily.

Market squid is an important commercial resource in California and is the largest California fishery by both volume landed and dollar value. Commonly employed fishing gear includes night-lights to attract them to the surface where they are netted using purse seines. Although market squid are extremely abundant, using large nets in their capture does result in a percentage of bycatch.

✦ ✦ ✦

After collection, market squid are iced, brought to shore, pumped into totes or trucks, and processed for fresh, frozen or canned sales. U.S. consumption is on the rise due to the increased awareness of the health benefits of seafood and to the more appealing market name of "calamari."

Cooked squid are mild, sweet, and tender—and are delicious fried, steamed, sautéed, baked or broiled.

Charred Squid Skewers on Garlic Toast with Arugula

CHEF TOM DOUGLAS, TOM DOUGLAS RESTAURANTS, Seattle, Washington

❖

2 pounds squid bodies, cleaned, with or without tentacles ▪ 12 or more 10-inch bamboo skewers, soaked in water for 30 minutes and drained ▪ FOR THE MARINADE: 3 tablespoons fresh flat leaf parsley, finely chopped ▪ 2 tablespoons fresh cilantro, finely chopped ▪ 2 tablespoons fresh lemon juice ▪ 2 teaspoons minced garlic ▪ 2 teaspoons paprika ▪ ¼ teaspoon cayenne pepper ▪ 2 teaspoons grated lemon zest ▪ ¾ teaspoon kosher salt ▪ ½ teaspoon freshly-ground black pepper ▪ ½ cup extra virgin olive oil ▪ FOR THE LEMON VINAIGRETTE: 1 tablespoon fresh lemon juice ▪ 2 teaspoons minced shallots ▪ 2 tablespoons extra virgin olive oil ▪ kosher salt and freshly-ground black pepper ▪ 1 fresh baguette ▪ 5 cups fresh arugula leaves, washed and dried with stems trimmed

If squid bodies have fins (thin flaps) attached, slice off and discard. Put the blade of the knife inside the squid body and carefully slice open so you have one flat piece. Cut this piece in half, lengthwise. You will have 2 squid pieces, shaped like 2 long, tapered rectangles. Using the knife, lightly score the inside of each rectangle in a crosshatch pattern, not cutting all the way through. Repeat this procedure with all the squid bodies. To skewer the squid, thread one rectangle, lengthwise, onto a bamboo skewer, followed by 2 tentacles (if using), then another rectangle. Continue this procedure until all the squid is used. TO MAKE THE MARINADE: Combine the ingredients in a bowl and whisk in the oil. Pour the marinade over the squid skewers, cover, and refrigerate for 30 minutes. TO MAKE THE LEMON VINAIGRETTE: Combine the ingredients and whisk in the olive oil. Season to taste with salt and pepper; reserve. TO MAKE THE GARLIC TOASTS: Cut a baguette on the diagonal into slices about ⅓-inch thick. Brush both sides with olive oil. Place slices under the broiler, turning once until golden and toasted. TO GRILL THE SQUID: Heat outdoor grill. Remove skewers from refrigerator and allow squid to come to room temperature. Shake off excess marinade and grill skewers over a hot fire, direct heat, with the lid off. Turn skewers several times until squid is cooked through, opaque, and charred in a few places. Do not overcook or squid will be tough. Remove skewers from grill. TO SERVE: Put the arugula in a bowl and toss with about 2 tablespoons of the Lemon Vinaigrette. Arrange the garlic toasts on a platter. Top each toast with some arugula salad. Put 2 squid skewers on top of each toast and drizzle the remaining vinaigrette over the skewers. *Serves six.*

Charred Squid Skewers on Garlic Toast with Arugula

Day Octopus

Octopus cyanea

Hawaii's resident day octopus matures within one year and lives no longer than 18 months, making them a very short-lived seafood item. Productivity is also high, with female octopi laying up to 700,000 eggs during their one and only breeding cycle.

The day octopus is a small, brown-and-tan mottled species which is found foraging on shallow and deepwater reefs in the Hawaiian Islands. Common names for this species include the Big Blue Octopus and Cyane's Octopus. Day octopus can reach a maximum arm span of two to three feet and a maximum weight of ten pounds. As its name implies, the day octopus is most active during daylight hours and rests in a shelter or "den" at night.

When selecting octopus, the day octopus from Hawaii is the preferred seafood choice because Hawaii's commercial and recreational octopus fisheries employ low-bycatch methods. Being a popular

Seafood WATCH

The day octopus from Hawaii is the preferred seafood choice because Hawaii's commercial and recreational octopus fisheries employ low-bycatch methods (spearfishing and lure-and-line fishing).

Since this particular octopus inhabits fragile coral reef ecosystems, and there has been no stock assessment or fisheries management plan in place, consumers should consider this "Good Alternatives."

For current fishery status, visit www.seafoodwatch.org

food item, the day octopus is harvested by local fishermen who catch them by hand, hook-and-line, or with the use of spears. The giant Pacific octopus and the European/African octopus, on the other hand, are not well regulated and are often caught using bottom trawls on vulnerable rocky-reef habitat. These species, and other species that are collected by harmful methods, should be avoided.

A relative of the squid, cuttlefish, and chambered nautilus, the day octopus is a highly mobile predator, using its eight arms to crawl swiftly across the bottom. Short, darting movements and fast escapes are made by jet propulsion as water is inhaled into the mantle cavity (gill chamber) and then forced out through the siphon. Day octopi can also escape detection by both prey and predators thanks to their ability to change skin color to match their surroundings.

Day octopus feed on crustaceans (shrimp, lobsters, crabs) and mollusks. They capture their prey with a swift pounce using the arms and webbing of their body. The mouth is located on the underside of the body, in the center of the arms. As the prey is held fast by the suckers, a toxin produced by the salivary glands is injected to paralyze the prey and liquefy its flesh. The octopus then uses its parrot-like beak to tear the softened meat into small bite-size pieces.

❖ ❖ ❖

In today's seafood markets, day octopus is available fresh or frozen, raw or cooked, and whole (cleaned and debeaked), or as octopus legs. The meat should be white and firm with a sweet, mild flavor.

Octopus with Green Papaya Slaw and Green Curry Vinaigrette

Octopus with Green Papaya Slaw and Green Curry Vinaigrette

CHEF TOM DOUGLAS, Etta's, Seattle, Washington

◆

FOR THE OCTOPUS AND SLAW: ½ pound cooked octopus (taiko), cut into ⅛-inch-thick slices ▪ 3 cups peeled and julienned green papaya (green papaya is a large, unripe papaya that is often used in Asian cooking. The flesh should be light green. Use a mandolin to get nice, thin julienne slices) ▪ 1 cup julienne carrots ▪ **FOR THE NUOC CHAM:** ¼ cup fresh lime juice ▪ 2 tablespoons sugar ▪ 2 tablespoons Asian fish sauce ▪ 2 tablespoons water ▪ 2 teaspoons chopped cilantro ▪ ½ teaspoon red pepper flakes ▪ ½ teaspoon finely chopped lemongrass, tender white part only ▪ **FOR THE GREEN CURRY VINAIGRETTE:** 2 tablespoons finely chopped lemongrass, tender white part only ▪ 2 tablespoons finely-chopped green onions ▪ ¼ cup chopped fresh basil ▪ 2 tablespoons chopped fresh cilantro ▪ 2 tablespoons chopped fresh mint ▪ 1 teaspoon peeled and grated fresh ginger ▪ ¼ teaspoon minced garlic ▪ 2 teaspoons Thai chile (or other hot chile), seeded and finely chopped ▪ ¼ cup rice wine vinegar ▪ 1½ teaspoons sugar ▪ 1½ teaspoons Asian fish sauce ▪ ¼ cup peanut oil, or vegetable oil ▪ lime wedges for garnish

To make the vinaigrette, combine the lemongrass, green onions, herbs, ginger, garlic, and chile in a food processor or blender and purée as finely as possible. Add the vinegar, sugar and fish sauce and process to combine. Remove to a small bowl and whisk in the peanut oil; reserve. Place the julienned green papaya and carrots in a bowl and toss with the Nuoc Cham. To make the Nuoc Cham, whisk together all the ingredients as noted above. **TO SERVE:** Mound the slaw on 6 plates. Arrange the octopus slices around each mound of slaw and drizzle some of the green curry vinaigrette around each salad. Garnish with lime wedges. *Serves six.*

Grilled Octopus with Yuzu Soy Vinaigrette

CHEF ROY YAMAGUCHI ROY'S, Honolulu, Hawaii

◆

14 ounces, fresh day octopus ▪ **FOR THE MARINADE:** 4 tablespoons green onions, minced ▪ 4 teaspoons ginger juice ▪ 4 tablespoons lemon juice ▪ 8 tablespoons soy sauce ▪ 8 teaspoons sugar ▪ 8 teaspoons saké ▪ 1 teaspoon shichimi ▪ **FOR THE YUZU VINAIGRETTE:** 1 tablespoon peanut oil ▪ 2 teaspoons ginger, grated ▪ 1 tablespoon onion chives, minced ▪ 4 tablespoons yuzu juice ▪ 2 tablespoons soy sauce ▪ 1 tablespoon olive oil ▪ **GARNISH:** ½ cup Japanese cucumber, thinly sliced ▪ ½ cup ogo (seaweed) ▪ 1 tablespoon masago caviar ▪ 1 head baby frisee lettuce (white part only)

Begin by combining all the marinade ingredients and marinate octopus for 15 to 20 minutes. While octopus is marinating, prepare the Yuzu Vinaigrette by whisking together all the ingredients in a bowl until combined; reserve. Next, grill the octopus between medium-rare to medium doneness for about 3 to 4 minutes per side. **TO SERVE:** Place the sliced cucumbers in the middle of 4 plates. Slice the grilled octopus very thin and place over the cucumbers. Place the baby frisee and ogo over the octopus and sprinkle with masago caviar. Mirror the plate with the vinaigrette. *Serves four.*

Red Sea Urchin

Stronglyocentrotus franciscanus

RED SEA URCHIN

The red sea urchin is among the longest living animals on Earth—they can live to be 100 years old, and some may reach 200 years or more. These older urchins aid in providing more young, which helps in creating a sustainable fishery. Historically, sea urchins had been considered a nuisance.

Sea urchins appeared on Earth around 500 million years ago. Sea urchins are found in every ocean of the world and over 700 different species have been identified. In North America, three species of urchins predominate—the red sea urchin, the smaller purple, and the green sea urchin. Red sea urchins are the principal commercial species.

A relative of the star fish, the red sea urchin is a spiny, hard-shelled animal that lives on the rocky seafloor from shallow waters to great depths. Their skin has hard, chalky plates called the test. Red sea urchins have a globular body with long spines that are used for protection, for moving, and for trapping drifting algae to eat.

Red sea urchins are harvested for their roe, called "uni," which is considered an aphrodisiac by some. Inside the sea urchin are five yellowish-orange strips arranged in a star-shaped pattern. These strips are the roe or uni. Uni has a very sweet flavor and delicate texture. It is generally consumed chilled. High-quality uni is mainly sold on auction at the major wholesale markets such as at the

Tsukiji Market in Tokyo. Factors affecting the price include freshness, color, shape, firmness, and taste. Uni is a delicacy in Japan and at sushi bars worldwide.

On the U.S. Pacific Coast, red, purple and green sea urchins are all commercially harvested. On the Atlantic Coast, only green sea urchins are commercially harvested. The green urchin is collected by dredges that drag along the ocean floor and often damage the bottom. The same is true with the purple urchin. Fortunately, the red sea urchin on the West coast, particularly in Central California, is commercially harvested by hand by local divers. Harvesting takes place at depths of five to 100 feet, with most dives taking place in 20 to 60 feet of water. Sea urchins are collected from the ocean bottom with a hand-held rake or hook and put into a hoop net bag or wire basket.

✦   ✦   ✦

Using permit and license requirements, control over fishing methods, seasonal closures, diver limitations, and minimum size requirements, the red sea urchin fishery is well managed by the California Department of Fish and Game, and is the best choice when selecting urchin.

Seafood WATCH

Based on current reports, the red sea urchin on the West coast, particularly in Central California, is commercially harvested by hand by local divers—a method considered eco-friendly because no bycatch is involved and the taking of juvenile urchins is prohibited. On the Atlantic Coast, green sea urchins are commercially harvested by dredges that drag along the ocean floor and often damage the bottom. Such urchins should be avoided. "Good Alternatives" with Pacific red sea urchins although this species has not yet been evaluated by the Seafood Watch Program.

For current fishery status, visit www.seafoodwatch.org

Red Sea Urchin "Uni" Shooter

Chef Kaz Sato, Kai Sushi, Santa Barbara, California

✦

2 to 3 pieces fresh sea urchin roe "uni" ▪ ½ ounce ponzu sauce ▪ (FOR HOMEMADE PONZU: mix equal parts of lemon juice ▪ rice vinegar ▪ water ▪ saké ▪ and a pinch of dry seaweed) ▪ 1 quail egg (yolk only) ▪ pinch of finely-sliced scallion (damp dry with paper towel) ▪ one pinch of chili daikon (chili daikon is simply chili sauce mixed with finely shredded white radish)

TO SERVE: Fill a shot glass half full with ponzu sauce. Add 2 or 3 pieces of fresh uni. Add yolk of egg, and top off with a pinch of scallions and chili daikon. *Serves one.*

Fresh Sea Urchin Roe with Lemon and Lime

Chef Keary Patrick Bevan, Seattle, Washington

✦

1 or 2 live red sea urchins ▪ shaved ice ▪ an assortment of crackers ▪ lemon and lime wedges

A sea urchin is 5 sided and round, as are all Echinoderms (starfish, urchins, brittle stars, etc.). The urchin's mouth is on the bottom. Using a pair of kitchen scissors, remove the top of the live urchin as you would do a pumpkin, and set aside. Remove the top carefully to avoid being injured by the spines and not to damage the delicate roe inside. It may be necessary to use an iron or knife to crack part of the shell before inserting the scissors. The urchin roe (or "uni") are the 5 yellow strips, resembling "little tongues," that run from top to bottom on the inside of the shell. Carefully run a small utensil like a butter knife under the roe along the inside of the shell to loosen it. Roe is incredibly fragile so try not to break it. If you break it into more than 2 pieces or smash it, toss the piece. The trick to eating urchin is to understand how delicate the roe is. Remove the intact pieces of roe and place in a chilled plastic dish (as heat will dissolve the roe). Using fingers or tweezers, clean each piece of roe by removing any particles, such as partly digested seaweed or plumbing for the urchin. When the roe is cleaned, it is important to give them a quick rinse in fresh water. The roe should be well drained, especially if they are not to be eaten immediately. TO SERVE: Hollow out the urchin shell, again like you would do a pumpkin, being careful not to break the spines. Fill the shell with shaved ice. Place the five strips of roe in a star-shaped pattern on the ice. Cover with the urchin top and place on a serving dish, accompanied with crackers and wedges of lemon and lime. *Serves two to four.*

Red Sea Urchin "Uni" Shooter

Jellyfish

Catostylus mosaicus and *Stomolophus meleagris*

JELLYFISH

Jellyfish consist of 95 percent water, and they have neither a brain, heart, nor other internal organs. Most jellyfish receive their energy by feeding on planktonic animals. The edible jellyfish is named after the fact that it is edible, and is an exotic delicacy in the Far East.

The Blue Jellyfish *(Catostylus mosaicus)* and the Cannonball Jellyfish *(Stomolophus meleagris)* are two common species of edible jellyfish. The blue jelly is found along the Australian eastern coast, while the cannonball jelly is collected in the waters off Florida. Jellyfish is a highly regarded delicacy in the Orient, where over 40 percent of jellyfish production is consumed.

In general, jellyfish vary in color but each has a large bell and tentacles. They have no mouth but there are many tiny openings in their tentacles that function as mouths. The tentacles also contain stinging cells and are used to capture tiny crustaceans and other plankton for food.

An important fact about jellyfish is the collagen they contain. The human body needs collagen to build cell tissue, cartilage, teeth and bones. For more than a thousand years, Asians have eaten jellyfish to treat high blood pressure, arthritis, and other diseases.

Jellyfish are harvested using a dip or scoop net. Massive congregations of jellyfish often occur during the summer months when water temperatures increase—creating a nuisance for fishermen targeting other seafood. Although they have some degree of mobility, jellyfish are often swept along by

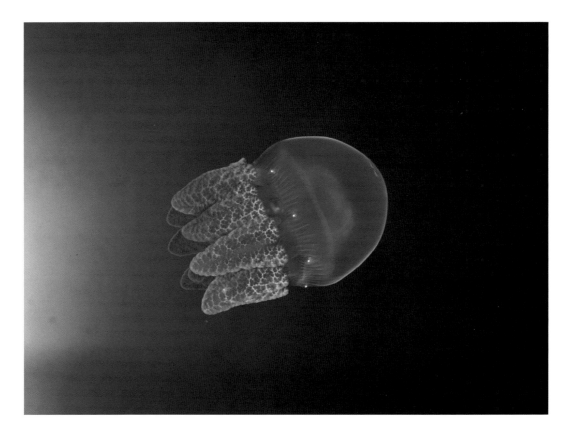

Seafood WATCH

Based on current reports, various species of edible jellyfish are harvested using dip or scoop nets. When massive congregations of jellyfish appear, particularly during summer months when water temperatures increase, fishermen will target them using large seine nets. "Good Alternatives" although edible jellyfish have not yet been evaluated by the Seafood Watch Program.

For current fishery status, visit www.seafoodwatch.org

currents and wind. Large numbers can be seen near shore and can be caught in bays with seine nets when conditions are right.

Processing must occur immediately after harvesting jellyfish. The tentacles are separated from the bell of the animal and cleaned to remove debris and mucus. A mixture of salt and alum is used to remove moisture in a series of drying stages, up to four of which are used for top quality jellyfish products.

◆ ◆ ◆

Once salted and dried, jellyfish still requires several steps by the consumer before it is ready to be served, including de-salting, cooking and rehydrating. On its own, jellyfish has no flavor, but after softening, boiling and marinating, jellyfish is a great addition to vegetables or salads.

Spicy Jellyfish Salad with Endive, Smelt Eggs and Avocado

Spicy Jellyfish Salad with Endive, Smelt Eggs and Avocado

CHEF KAZ SATO, KAI SUSHI, Santa Barbara, California

✦

2 ounces jellyfish, chopped lengthwise ▪ 1 large pinch of kaiware (radish sprouts; small bunch; 10 to 12 leaves) ▪ fresh spinach ▪ ¼ cup chopped sweet onion (white or red) ▪ 1 large pinch of green onions or scallions (julienne style) ▪ 2 tablespoons cucumber (julienne style) ▪ 1 fried wanton skin ▪ salt and pepper to taste ▪ olive oil (as needed) ▪ sesame seeds (as needed) ▪ smelt eggs (as needed) ▪ FOR GARNISH: 4 endive leaves ▪ 1 avocado (sliced) ▪ 2 tablespoons smelt eggs

Mix together jellyfish, kaiware, spinach leaves, sweet onion, cucumber, and add salt, pepper, and olive oil to taste; set aside. Deep fry the wanton skin. TO SERVE: Place wanton skin in center of dish. Place a large scoop of salad inside the wanton skin. On top of salad, add ½ teaspoon smelt eggs, and sprinkle sesame seeds over salad. TO GARNISH: Add four endive leaves around salad. Inside each leaf, place a slice of avocado and ½ teaspoon of smelt eggs. *Serves one or two.*

Sesame Marinated Jellyfish

MS. MELISSA HOPE, TONMO.COM—*The Octopus News Magazine*, New York, New York

✦

½ pound prepared shredded jellyfish ▪ 2 teaspoons light soy sauce ▪ 3 tablespoons sesame oil ▪ 2 teaspoons white rice vinegar ▪ 2 teaspoons sugar ▪ 3 tablespoons white sesame seeds, toasted

Rinse the jellyfish well under cold running water and drain. Place jellyfish in a stainless steel bowl and cover with boiling water. Let the jellyfish sit in the water for about 15 minutes or until tender. Drain and continue to soak at least 6 times in several changes of cold water. Drain thoroughly and blot dry with paper towels; set aside. In a small bowl, mix soy sauce, sesame oil, vinegar and sugar. Add the jellyfish and toss well in the sauce; let it sit for at least 30 minutes. TO SERVE: Plate the marinated jellyfish and garnish with toasted sesame seeds just before serving. *Serves two to four.*

SEAFOOD DISTRIBUTORS

Can't find sustainable seafood at your local supermarket? No need to panic. There are a number of seafood distributors around the nation who will ship right to your doorstep. Below is a list of names to get you going.

Rainbow Trout (farmed)
Clear Springs Foods
Buhl, Idaho
800-635-8211
www.clearprings.com

Arctic Char (farmed)
Northern Treasures
Whitehorse, Yukon Canada
867-668-4506
www.arcticchar.com

Catfish (farmed)
Simmons Farm Raised Catfish
Yazoo City, Mississippi
662-746-5687
www.simmonscatfish.com

Crayfish (farmed)
Louisiana Crawfish Company
Natchitoches, Louisiana
888-522-7292
www.lacrawfish.com

White Sturgeon &
White Sturgeon Caviar (farmed)
Stolt Sea Farm / Sterling
Sacramento, California
916-991-4420
www.stoltseafarm.com

Sardines
Raffield Fisheries Inc
Port St. Joe, Florida
850-229-8229
www.raffieldfisheries.com

Pacific Cod
Ed's Kasilof Seafoods
Kenai Peninsula, Alaska
800-982-2377
www.kasilofseafoods.com

New Zealand Cod (Hoki)
Slade Gorton & Company
Boston, Massachusetts
800-225-1573
www.sladegorton.com

Sockeye Salmon (wild)
Ed's Kasilof Seafoods
Kenai Peninsula, Alaska
800-982-2377
www.kasilofseafoods.com

Chinook Salmon (wild)
Ed's Kasilof Seafoods
Soldotna, Alaska
800-982-2377
www.kasilofseafoods.com

Coho Salmon (wild)
Ed's Kasilof Seafoods
Soldotna, Alaska
800-982-2377
www.kasilofseafoods.com

Pacific Halibut
Ed's Kasilof Seafoods
Soldotna, Alaska
800-982-2377
www.kasilofseafoods.com

Spanish Mackerel
Raffield Fisheries Inc
Port St. Joe, Florida
850-229-8229
www.raffieldfisheries.com

Albacore
Catalina Offshore Products
San Diego, California
619-297-9797
www.catalinaop.com

Yellowfin Tuna
Catalina Offshore Products
San Diego, California
619-297-9797
www.catalinaop.com

Mahi Mahi
ChefShop.com, Inc.
Seattle, Washington
206-286-9988
www.chefshop.com

Wahoo
Key West Seafood.com
Key West, Florida
800-292-9853
www.keywestseafood.com

Dungeness Crab
Oregon Dungeness Crab Commission
Coos Bay, Oregon
541-267-5810
www.oregondungeness.org

King Crab
Ed's Kasilof Seafoods
Soldotna, Alaska
800-982-2377
www.kasilofseafoods.com

Fisherman's Express Alaska Seafoods
Anchorage, Alaska
888-926-3474
www.fishermansexpress.com

Blue Crab
The Crab Place
Crisfield, Maryland
877-EAT-CRAB

Florida Stone Crab
Keys Fisheries, Inc.
Marathon, Florida
305-743-6727

Pink Shrimp
Fisherman's Express Alaska Seafoods
Anchorage, Alaska
888-926-3474
www.fishermansexpress.com

Alaska Spot Prawns
Fisherman's Express Alaska Seafoods
Anchorage, Alaska
888-926-3474
www.fishermansexpress.com

California Spiny Lobster
Coastal Catch
Santa Barbara, CA
805-730-1941

Main Lobster
Coastal Catch
Santa Barbara, CA
805-730-1941

Red Abalone (farmed)
The Abalone Farm
Cayucos, California
877-367-2271
www.abalonefarm.com

Pacific Clams (farmed)
Penn Cove Shellfish, LLC
Coupeville, Washington
360-678-4803
www.penncoveshellfish.com

Blue & Mediterranean Mussels (farmed)
Penn Cove Shellfish, LLC
Coupeville, Washington
360-678-4803
www.penncoveshellfish.com

West Coast Oysters (farmed)
Penn Cove Shellfish, LLC
Coupeville, Washington
360-678-4803
www.penncoveshellfish.com

Atlantic Bay Scallops (farmed)
Farm 2 Market
Roscoe, New York
800-663-4326

Atlantic Sea Scallops
Farm 2 Market
Roscoe, New York
800-663-4326

Market Squid
Catalina Offshore Products
San Diego, California
619-297-9797
www.catalinaop.com

Day Octopus
Catalina Offshore Products
San Diego, California
619-297-9797
www.catalinaop.com

Red Sea Urchin
Catalina Offshore Products
San Diego, California
619-297-9797
www.catalinaop.com

ACKNOWLEDGMENTS

The author would like to personally thank the following individuals and organizations
for their generous support and assistance with this cookbook

Tom Petrie, Andrea Donner, and the entire staff at Willow Creek Press; Jeff Tucker and Kevin Hossler; Kelsey Donwen; Elizabeth Watson; Julie Packard, Hank Armstrong, Ken Peterson, Jennifer Dianto, Ginger Hopkins, Kris Ingram, and the rest of the helpful staff at the Monterey Bay Aquarium; Jean-Michel Cousteau, Barbara LaPiana, and the entire team at Ocean Futures Society; the National Oceanic and Atmospheric Administration/ Department of Commerce (NOAA) and the generous individuals willing to share their remarkable images and observations with America and the rest of the world, particularly William B. Folsom, P.R. Nelson, J.M. Olson, Edward J. Pastula, Dr. Aleksey Zuyev, Mary Hollinger, Nance S. Trueworthy, Commander John Bortnia and Jeff Kietzmann; Rex Browning for his editorial assistance; Visuals Unlimited; Diane Somers, Alaska Division of Tourism, and the Alaska Division of Community and Business Development; Chris Howard, Clear Springs Foods; Joy & David McGraw, Louisiana Crawfish Company; Seger Collier, Simmons Farm Raised Catfish; Lanny Anderson, Northern Treasures; Kim North, Stolt Sea Farm California; Kevin Fitzsimmons, University of Arizona and The American Tilapia Association; the Canadian Sablefish Association; Tom Elliott, Slade Gorton; Glenn McGill, Sanford Sustainable Fisheries; Jeff & Jim Trujillo, Ed's Kasilof Seafoods; the Alaska Seafood Marketing Institute; Eugene Raffield Jr., Raffield Fisheries; Charles H. Bronson and the Florida Dept of Agriculture & Consumer Services; Dave Rudie, Catalina Offshore Products; Howard Deese, State of Hawaii, Department of Business, Economic Development & Tourism, Ocean Resources Branch; Eliza Ward, ChefShop.com; Captain Mark Phillips, Key West Seafood.com; Wreckfish fisherman Samuel Ray; Jeff Riggs, Fisherman's Express Alaska Seafoods; Gary Graves, Keys Fisheries Inc; Nick Furman, Oregon Dungeness Crab Commission; Greg Cain, The Crab Place; Kent Schiff, Coastal Catch; Lobster fishermen Bob & Raleigh Sharp; Brad Buckley, The Abalone Farm; Ian Jefferds, Penn Cove Shellfish, LLC; Marshall Shnider, Farm 2 Market; Lazy Acres; The Bay Café; Gelson's Market, Kanaloa Seafood . . . and last but not least, a big thank you to all the supportive chefs and restaurants for their extreme generosity in providing the sumptuous seafood recipes.

PHOTOGRAPHY CREDITS

Tucker + Hossler (cover; pgs 3, 7, 8, 21, 22, 25, 28, 33, 36, 38, 41, 51, 55, 58, 60, 63, 64, 66, 71, 74, 79, 82, 84, 87, 90, 92, 95, 98, 103, 104, 106, 108, 111, 112, 114, 116, 119, 122, 127, 130, 135, 136, 138, 140, 143, 145, 146, 149, 152, 157, 160, 162, 165, 168, 173, 174, 176, 178, 181, 183, 184, 187, 188, 190, 192, 195, 196, 198, 200, 203, 204, 206, 211, 212, 214, 219, 222); **National Oceanic and Atmospheric Administration/Department of Commerce–NOAA** (pgs 31, 53, 56, 57, 65, 77, 81, 85, 89, 97, 101, 105, 117, 121, 125, 129, 133, 137, 140, 141, 150, 159, 171, 179, 201, 205, 209); **James O. Fraioli** (cover; pgs 4, 5, 6, 9, 89, 93, 109, 113, 132, 163, 175, 179, 209, 213, 216, 217, 221, 224, 225, 228, 230, 231, 232); **Visuals Unlimited** (pgs 8, 9, 34, 39, 53, 57, 61, 96, 117, 120, 125, 133, 141, 158, 171, 185, 201, 205, 213); **The Monterey Bay Aquarium** (pgs 14, 16, 43, 52, 61, 76, 101, 166, 170, 220); **Alaska Division of Tourism & the Alaska Division of Community and Business Development** (pgs 18, 19, 27, 73, 88, 93, 97, 100, 151, 167, 227, 229); **Fisherman's Express Alaska Seafoods** (pgs 151, 154, 155); **Penn Cove Shellfish, LLC** (pgs 189, 193, 197); **Oregon Dungeness Crab Commission** (pgs 19, 47); **Stolt Sea Farm California** (pgs 39, 43); **Canadian Sablefish Association** (pgs 68, 69); **Jim J. Fraioli** (pgs 121, 155); **Lanny Anderson, Northern Treasures** (pgs 26, 27); **Washington State Tourism, Department of Community, Trade and Economic Development** (pgs 77, 81); **Visit Florida Media Image Library** (pgs 105, 137); **Terry Steven Holt, Aigrette Photography & www.stockpix.com** (pgs 6, 30); **Tom Ordway, Ocean Futures Society** (pg 12); **Jason Eggbert** (cover); **Clear Springs Foods** (pg 23); **Simmons Farm Raised Catfish** (pg 31); **Louisiana Crawfish Company** (pg 35); **Kevin Fitzsimmons, University of Arizona and The American Tilapia Association** (pg 47); **Sanford Sustainable Fisheries** (pg 73); **State of Hawaii, Department of Business, Economic Development & Tourism, Ocean Resources Branch** (pg 128); **The Abalone Farm** (pg 185); **Daniel W. Gotshall, Sea Challengers Inc** (pg 80); **Corel Images** (pg 208); **Hann, Wreford Hann Photography Ltd** (pg 72); **John E. Randall** (pg 124).

SPECIES INDEX

Abalone
    Red Abalone, 184–186
Albacore, 17, 116–118
Anchovy
    Northern Anchovy, 52–54

Bass
    Chilean Sea Bass, 17
    Striped Bass, 17, 112–115
    White Sea Bass, 108–110

Catfish, 17, 30–32
Caviar, 17, 42–45
Char
    Artic Char, 26–29
Clams, 17, 188–190
    Littleneck Clams, 191
    Steamer Clams, 191
Cod, 17
    Black Cod, 68–71
    New Zealand Cod, 72–75
    Pacific Cod, 64–67
Crab, 17
    Alaska Red King Crab, 17, 150–153
    Blue Crab, 17, 158–161
    Dungeness Crab, 17, 146–148
    Florida Stone Crab, 17, 162–164
    Green Mangrove Crab, 163–164
    Snow Crab, 17, 154–156
Crayfish, 34–37

Flounder, 17

Grouper, 17

Halibut, 17
    Pacific Halibut, 17, 88–91

Herring
    Atlantic Herring, 56–59
Hoki, 72–75
    Red Hoki, 75

Jellyfish, 220–223

Lobster,
    California Spiny Lobster, 17, 174–177
    Maine Lobster, 17, 178–180

Mackerel
    Spanish Makerel, 104–107
Mahi Mahi, 132–134
Monkfish, 17
Moonfish, *see Opah*
Mussels, 17
    Blue Mussels, 192–194

Octopus
    Day Octopus, 212–215
Opah, 128–131
Orange Roughy, 17
Oysters, 17
    West Coast Oysters, 196–199

Pollock, 17
Prawn
    Alaska Spot Prawn, 170–172

Rockfish, 17

Sablefish, 68–71
Salmon, 17
    Chinook Salmon, 100–102
    Coho Salmon, 96–99
    Sockeye Salmon, 92–94

Sanddabs, 80–83
Sardines, 17
    Pacific Sardines, 60–62
Scallops, 17
    Atlantic Bay Scallops, 17, 200–202
Sea Scallops, 17
    Atlantic Sea Scallops, 204–207
Sea Urchin
    Red Sea Urchin, 216–218
Shark, 17
Shrimp, 17
    Pink Shrimp, 166–169
Snails, *see Red Abalone*
Snapper, Red/Vermilion, 17
Sole, 17
    Dover Sole, 17, 76–78
    Petrale Sole, 17, 84–86
Squid, 17
    Market Squid, 208–210
Sturgeon, 17
    White Sturgeon, 38–40
        Caviar, 42–45
Swordfish, 17

Tilapia, 17, 46–48
Trevally Jack, 124–126
Trout
    Rainbow Trout, 17, 22–24
Tuna
    Albacore, 17, 116–118
    Bigeye Tuna, 17
    Bluefin Tuna, 17
    canned, 17
    Yellowfin Tuna, 17, 120–123

Wahoo, 136–139
Wreckfish, 140–142